THE SECRET OF THE

A Lamaist Vajry-Mandala, to be studied in preparation
for meditation.

THE SECRET OF
THE GOLDEN FLOWER
A Chinese Book of Life

Translated and explained by
RICHARD WILHELM

with a Foreword and Commentary by
C. G. JUNG

and part of the Chinese meditation text
THE BOOK OF CONSCIOUSNESS AND LIFE
with a Foreword by
SALOME WILHELM

HarperOne
An Imprint of HarperCollins*Publishers*

BOSTON   NEW YORK

First published in the United States 1931

New, revised and augmented
edition published in 1962

www.harpercollins.com

Translated from the German by
Cary F. Baynes

Library of Congress Catalog Card Number: 62-10499
ISBN 978-0-15-679980-5 (Harvest: pbk.)
ISBN 0-15-679980-4 (Harvest: pbk.)

Type set in Weiss
Printed in the United States of America

23 24 25 26 27 LBC 29 28 27 26 25

CONTENTS

A DISCUSSION OF THE TEXT BY RICHARD WILHELM

TRANSLATION OF THE T'AI I CHIN HUA TSUNG CHIH

THE HUI MING CHING

COMMENTARY BY C. G. JUNG

Contents

TRANSLATOR'S PREFACE

THE ORIGINAL GERMAN EDITION of the *The Secret of the Golden Flower*, of which the following is the authorized English translation, appeared first in the autumn of 1929. On March 1, 1930, Richard Wilhelm died. In May, 1930, memorial services were held in Munich, and Jung was asked to deliver the principal address. The latter finds an appropriate place in the English version,[1] which is published a year or more after the co-author's death. The address will be welcomed, not only for what it tells the reader of Wilhelm but for the further light it throws on the standpoint of the East.

The relation of the West to Eastern thought is a highly paradoxical and confusing one. On the one side, as Jung points out, the East creeps in among us by the back door of the unconscious and strongly influences us in perverted forms, and on the other we repel it with violent prejudice as concerned with a fine-spun metaphysics that is poisonous to the scientific mind.

If anyone is in doubt as to how far the East influences us in secret ways, let him but briefly investigate the fields covered to-day by what is called 'occult thought'. Millions of people are included in these movements and Eastern ideas dominate all of them. Since there is nowhere any sign of a psychological understanding of the phenomena on which they are based, they undergo a complete twisting and are a real menace in our world.

A partial realization of what is going on in this direction, together with the Westerner's native ignorance and mistrust of the world of inner experience, builds up the prejudice against

[1] See Appendix, p. 138.

the reality of Eastern wisdom. When the wisdom of the Chinese is laid before a Westerner, he is very likely to ask with a sceptical lift of the brows why such profound wisdom did not save China from its present horrors. Of course, he does not stop to think that the Chinese asks with an equal scepticism why the much-boasted scientific knowledge of the West, not to mention its equally boasted Christian ethics, did not save it from a World War. But as a matter of fact, present conditions in China do not invalidate Chinese wisdom, nor did the Great War prove the futility of science. In both cases we are dealing with the negative sides of principles under which East and West live, and it has not yet been given, either to individuals or to nations, to manage the vices of their virtues. Mastery of the inner world, with a relative contempt for the outer, must inevitably lead to great catastrophes. Mastery of the outer world, to the exclusion of the inner, delivers us over to the demonic forces of the latter and keeps us barbaric despite all outward forms of culture. The solution cannot be found either in deriding Eastern spirituality as impotent or by mistrusting science as a destroyer of humanity. We have to see that the spirit must lean on science as its guide in the world of reality, and that science must turn to the spirit for the meaning of life.

Such is the point of view established in this book. Through the combined efforts of Wilhelm and Jung we have for the first time a way of understanding and appreciating Eastern wisdom which satisfies all sides of our minds. It has been taken out of metaphysics and placed in psychological experience. We approach it with an entirely new tool, and are protected from the perversions the East undergoes at the hands of the cult-mongers of the West. At the same time, its meaning for us is greatly deepened when we know that, despite the gulf separating us from the East, we follow exactly similar paths when once we give heed to the inner world.

But this book not only gives us a new approach to the East, it also strengthens the point of view evolving in the West with respect to the psyche. The reshaping of values in progress to-day forces the modern man out of a nursery-world of collective traditions into an adult's world of individual choice. He knows that his choice and his fate now turn upon his understanding of himself. Much has been taught him in recent years about the hitherto unsuspected elements in his psyche, but the emphasis is all too often on the static side alone, so that he finds himself possessed of little more than an inventory of contents, the nature of which serves to burden him with a sense of weariness rather than to spur him on to master the problems that confront him. Yet it is precisely the need of understanding himself in terms of change and renewal which most grips the imagination of modern man. Having seen the world of matter disappear before his scientific eye and reappear as a world of energy, he comes to ask himself a bold question: Does he not contain within his psyche a store of unexplored forces, which, if rightly understood, would give him a new vision of himself and help safeguard the future for him? In this book his question is answered from two widely different sources, Chinese yoga and analytical psychology. Stripped of its archaic setting, *The Secret of the Golden Flower* is the secret of the powers of growth latent in the psyche, and these same powers as they reveal themselves in the minds of Western men also form the theme of Jung's commentary. In the commentary he has shown the profound psychological development resulting from the right relationship to the forces within the psyche.

*   *   *

In the German edition Jung's commentary comes first, followed by Wilhelm's exposition of the text, and then by the text itself. At Jung's request, the order has been changed so that his commentary follows the text.

The Chinese words in this edition are in the Anglicized form. For making the necessary transcriptions, I am indebted both to Mr. Arthur Waley and to Colonel F. C. C. Egerton. The latter has been kind enough to give his personal attention to the editing of my manuscript.

As a possible aid in keeping in mind the relationships between the various Chinese concepts such as *hsing-ming*, *kuei-shen*, etc., I have added two summaries, one written and one diagrammatic.

Fortunately for me, I have made this translation under the supervision of Dr. Jung, and to that fact, and to the further aid I have received from Mrs. Jung, I owe any success I may have had in meeting the difficulties presented.

It has also been my privilege to have the completed manuscript read and criticized by Dr. Erla Rodakiewicz, and for her invaluable assistance I am deeply grateful.

CARY F. BAYNES

Zürich
March, 1931

TRANSLATOR'S NOTE TO THE NEW, REVISED EDITION

Thirty years have passed since the appearance of the first English edition of *The Secret of the Golden Flower*. A second World War has been fought and a third World War looms as a possibility. Man expends his energy upon the outer world without let or hindrance. In the midst of this extraversion, the 'continent of the spirit' recedes on the horizon. Does it still exist? The new edition of this book is an affirmative answer. It reminds us that man never really loses his vision of the 'continent of the spirit' and that the conquest of 'inner space', the understanding of the psyche, will remain the ultimate human goal. C. G. Jung, whose work was given wholly to that goal, died in 1961. Readers of this new edition will see in it a memorial to him as co-author of the book.

★ ★ ★

To the fifth German edition of *The Secret of the Golden Flower* several pages from another Chinese text on yoga closely related to that of the *Golden Flower* have been added. It is the *Hui Ming Ching*, or *Book of Consciousness and Life*. This new material now appears for the first time in English, and with it an introductory note by Salome Wilhelm containing a brief but important comment by her husband on the *Hui Ming Ching*. Another piece of new material appearing in English for the first time is Jung's Foreword to the second German edition.

Revision has brought about some radical changes in terminology in this edition. On the advice of Hellmut Wilhelm, *hsing*, which was translated as 'essence' (*Wesen*), has been changed to 'essence of human nature', or, briefly, 'human nature'. *Hsing*, very often co-ordinated with *ming*, life, like the latter, is a cosmic principle. It is, of course, startling to the Western reader to think of human nature in those terms, but the idea is fundamental to Chinese philosophy. A third world principle, *hui*, has importance in the new edition because of the *Hui Ming Ching*. *Hui*, consciousness, is related to *hsing*, human nature, but is not identical with it. A link in common is that both are opposites of *ming*, life, but they are separate concepts in Chinese thought.

Another important change in the translation, also made at the instance of Hellmut Wilhelm, is the substitution of 'energy' for 'force' (*Kraft*). 'Backward-flowing energy' is an example.

The translation has been carefully revised and checked for possible inaccuracies. Hellmut Wilhelm's assistance in the revision of the part of the book written by his father has led to many improvements besides those mentioned above. I am also indebted to him for the material in a number of new footnotes initialled by him, and for the statements concerning the relationship of *hsing*, *ming*, and *hui*.

My daughter, Ximena de Angulo, has given me indispensable aid with respect to the revision of the book as a whole.

CARY F. BAYNES

Morris, Connecticut
1961

FOREWORD
TO THE SECOND GERMAN EDITION

MY DECEASED FRIEND, Richard Wilhelm, the co-author of this book, sent me the text of *The Secret of the Golden Flower* at a time that was critical for my own work. I had been occupied with the investigation of the processes of the collective unconscious since the year 1913, and had obtained results that seemed to me questionable in more than one respect. They not only lay far beyond everything known to 'academic' psychology but also overstepped the borders of medical, strictly personal, psychology. These findings had to do with an extensive phenomenology, to which hitherto known categories and methods could no longer be applied. My results, based on fifteen years of effort, seemed inconclusive, because no possible comparison offered itself. I knew of no realm of human experience with which I might have backed up my findings with some degree of assurance. The only analogies—and these, I must say, were far removed in time—I found scattered through the reports of heresiologists. This connection did not in any way ease my task; on the contrary, it made it more difficult, because the Gnostic systems consist only in small part of immediate psychic experiences, the greater part being speculative and systematizing revisions. Since we possess only very few detailed texts, and since most of what is known comes from the reports of Christian opponents, we have, to say the least, an inadequate knowledge of the history, as well as of the contents, of this confused and strange literature, so difficult to encompass. Moreover, considering the fact that a period of not less than from seventeen hundred to eighteen hundred years separates the present from that past, support from that field seemed to me extraordinarily risky. Again, the connections were in part of a secondary character, and left gaps in the main issue which made it impossible for me to make use of the Gnostic material.

The text that Wilhelm sent me helped me out of this embarrassment. It contained exactly those pieces which I had sought for in vain among the Gnostics. Thus the text became a welcome opportunity to publish, at least in provisional form, some of the essential results of my investigations.

At that time it seemed unimportant to me that *The Secret of the Golden Flower* is not only a Taoist text of Chinese yoga but also an alchemical tract. However, a subsequent, deeper study of Latin tracts has corrected my outlook and shown me that the alchemical nature of the text is of prime significance. But this, to be sure, is not the place to go into more details about that point. I shall only emphasize the fact that it was the text of *The Golden Flower* that first put me in the direction of the right track. For we have in medieval alchemy the long-sought connecting-link between Gnosis and the processes of the collective unconscious, observable to us to-day in modern man.[1]

I take this opportunity to point out certain misunderstandings to which even well-informed readers of this book fell victim. Not infrequently people thought that my purpose in publishing the book was to put into the hands of the public a method of achieving happiness. In total misapprehension of all that I say in my commentary, such readers tried to imitate the 'method' described in the Chinese text. Let us hope that these representatives of spiritual profundity were few in number!

Another misunderstanding gave rise to the opinion that, in the commentary, I had pictured to a certain extent my psycho-

[1] The reader will find more about this in two essays published by me in the *Eranos Jahrbuch* 1936 and 1937. (This material can now be found in C. G. Jung, *Psychology and Alchemy*, Bollingen Series XII, London and New York, 1953. C. F. B.)

therapeutic method, which, it was said, consisted in my suggesting to my patients Eastern ideas for therapeutic purposes. I do not believe that there is anything in my commentary lending itself to that sort of superstition. In any case such an opinion is altogether erroneous, and is based on the widespread conception that psychology is an invention for a definite purpose and not an empirical science. To this category belongs the equally superficial as well as unintelligent opinion that the idea of the collective unconscious is 'metaphysical'. It is a question of an empirical concept to be put alongside the concept of instinct, as is obvious to anyone who will read with some attention.

I have added to this second edition the address in honour of Richard Wilhelm given by me at the memorial celebration, May 10, 1930, in Munich. It has already been published in the first English edition of 1931.[1]

C. G. JUNG

FOREWORD
TO THE FIFTH GERMAN EDITION

TO THIS EDITION there has been added the translation of the introductory portion of another meditation text stemming from a tradition similar to that of which *The Secret of the Golden Flower* is part, and appearing with the latter in the Chinese edition. Richard Wilhelm wrote the following brief introduction to this meditation text in 1926:

'The *Hui Ming Ching*, or *Book of Consciousness and Life*, was written by Liu Hua-yang in the year 1794. The author was born in the province of Kiangsi, and later became a monk in the monastery of the Double Lotus Flower (*Shuang-lien-ssu*) in the province of Anhui. The translation is from a new edition of a thousand copies printed with *The Secret of the Golden*

[1] *The Secret of the Golden Flower*, London and New York, 1931.

Flower in 1921 by a man with the pseudonym of Hui-chen-tzu ("he who has become conscious of truth").

'The text combines Buddhist and Taoist directions for meditation. The basic view is that at birth the two spheres of the psyche, consciousness and the unconscious, become separated. Consciousness is the element marking what is separated off, individualized, in a person, and the unconscious is the element that unites him with the cosmos. The unification of the two elements via meditation is the principle upon which the work is based. The unconscious must be inseminated by consciousness being immersed in it. In this way the unconscious is activated and thus, together with an enriched consciousness, enters upon a supra-personal mental level in the form of a spiritual rebirth. This rebirth then leads first to a progressing inner differentiation of the conscious state into autonomous thought structures. However, the conclusion of the meditation leads of necessity to the wiping out of all differences in the final integrated life, which is free of opposites.'

The German translation [of this meditation text] first appeared in the third volume of the *Chinesische Blätter für Wissenschaft und Kunst*, Darmstadt, 1926, pp. 104-114, the translator being L. C. Lo. Dr. Lo was at that time a collaborator of Richard Wilhelm's and Secretary of the China Institute in Frankfurt am Main. The translation was made at the suggestion of Richard Wilhelm and was revised by him, so that in its present form it closely approximates the style of the translation of *The Secret of the Golden Flower*. Inasmuch as the *Chinesische Blätter* had been brought out in a very limited edition, it seemed fitting to take this opportunity of making the text available to a wider circle of readers.

SALOME WILHELM

1957

A DISCUSSION OF THE TEXT

BY

RICHARD WILHELM

ORIGIN AND CONTENTS OF THE T'AI I CHIN HUA TSUNG CHIH

1. ORIGINS OF THE BOOK

THE BOOK comes from an esoteric circle in China. For a long time it was transmitted orally, and then in writing; the first printing is from the Ch'ien-lung period (eighteenth century). Finally a thousand copies of it were reprinted in Peking in 1920, together with the *Hui Ming Ching*, and were distributed among a small group of people who, in the opinion of the editor, understood the questions discussed. That is how I was able to get a copy. The new printing and circulation of the little book was due to a religious reawakening growing out of the exigencies of the political and economic conditions in China. There have been formed a series of secret sects whose effort is to achieve, by the practice of secret traditions from ancient times, a state of the psyche lifting them above all the misery of life. The methods used are magical writing, prayer, sacrifice, etc., and, in addition to these, mediumistic *séances*, widely prevalent in China, by means of which direct connection with the gods and the dead is sought. Experiments are also made with the planchette,[1] the flying spirit pencil as the Chinese call it.

But side by side with these practices there exists an esoteric movement which has devoted itself with energy to the psycho-

---

[1] It is a curious fact that the man who circulated this text had written for him by the planchette a preface by Lü-tsu, an adept of the T'ang dynasty [A.D. 618-907], to whom these teachings are accredited. However, this preface deviates very widely from the thoughts given in the book; it is flat and meaningless, like the majority of such productions.

3

logical method, that is meditation, or the practice of yoga. The followers of this method, in contradistinction to the European 'yogis' to whom these Eastern practices are only a form of sport, achieve, almost without exception, the central experience. Thus it can be said that, as far as the Chinese psyche is concerned, a completely assured method of attaining definite psychic experiences is available. (It must be noted that, as C. G. Jung very correctly points out, the Chinese mentality, at least up to very recent times, has been essentially different in some fundamental respects from that of Europeans.) Besides the release from the fetters of an illusory outer world, there are many other goals striven for by the different sects. Those on the highest level use this release by meditation for the purpose of seeking the Buddhist nirvana, or, as for example in the present book, they teach that by the union of the spiritual principle in men to the correlated psychogenic forces one can prepare for the possibility of life after death, not merely as a shadow-being doomed to dissolution but as a conscious spirit. In addition, and often in connection with this idea, there are schools of thought which try by means of this meditation to exert a psychic influence on certain processes of the sympathetic nervous system. (As Europeans we would speak here of the endocrine glandular system.) This influence strengthens, rejuvenates, and normalizes the life-processes, so that even death will be overcome in such a way that it fits in as a harmonious ending to life. That is to say, the spiritual principle, now fitted for an independent continuation of life in the spirit-body, created out of its own energy-system, deserts the earthly body, which remains behind as a drying shell like that shed by a cicada.

The lower strata of these sects have sought in this way to acquire magic powers, the ability to expel evil spirits and diseases, and here talismans, oral and written charms play their part. This sort of thing may lead to occasional mass psychoses which then work themselves out in religious or political unrest, as shown, for example, in the Boxer movement. Recently, the ever-present syncretistic tendency of Taoism has been shown in the fact that within such organizations, members of all the five world-religions (Confucianism, Taoism, Buddhism, Mohammedanism, and Christianity, even Judaism comes in occasionally for special mention) are included without having to break away from their respective religious congregations.

Having thus briefly described the background out of which such movements have grown up in our time, a word must be said as to the sources from which the teachings of the present book arise. Very remarkable discoveries come to light, and we find that these precepts are much older than their written form. The *T'ai I Chin Hua Tsung Chih*[1] can be traced back to the seventeenth century as having been printed from wooden tablets. The editor describes having found an incomplete copy dating from that time in the Liu-li-ch'ang, the old street of dealers in books and antiquities in Peking, and tells how he filled it out later from a friend's book. But the oral tradition goes back even further than that, to the Religion of the Golden Elixir of Life (*Chin-tan-chiao*), which developed in the T'ang period in the eighth century. The founder is said to have been the well-known Taoist adept, Lü Yen[2] (Lü Tung-pin), counted later by folk-lore as one of the eight immortals, about whom in the course of time a rich store of myths has gathered. This sect, like all religions, native and foreign, met with tolerance and favour in the T'ang period and spread widely, but, as it was always an esoteric and secret religion, in the course of time it began to suffer persecution because of members being suspected of

---

[1] *The Secret of the Golden Flower* (*T'ai I Chin Hua Tsung Chih*), the title of which was changed to *Ch'ang Sheng Shu* (*The Art of Prolonging Human Life*) by the Chinese publisher of the edition used here.

[2] Born *circa* A.D. 796. (H. W.)

political intrigues. Again and again its adherents were persecuted by a hostile government, lastly, in an extremely cruel way by the Manchus, just before their own fall.[1] Many members have turned to the Christian religion, and all, even if they have not actually entered the church, are very friendly towards it.

Our book gives the best available account of the religion of the Golden Elixir of Life. The sayings are attributed to Lü Yen, whose other name was Lü Tung-pin, or Lü, the Guest of the Cavern. In the book he is introduced as the patriarch Lü, Lü-tsu. He lived at the end of the eighth and at the beginning of the ninth century. A later commentary on his sayings has been added, but it springs from the same tradition.

Whence did Lü get his esoteric, secret lore? He himself attributes its origin to Kuan Yin-hsi, the Master Yin-hsi of the Pass (Kuan, i.e. Han-ku Pass), for whom, according to tradition, Lao-tse wrote down his *Tao Te Ching*. As a matter of fact, there are to be found in the system a great many thoughts taken from the esoteric, veiled, mystical teaching in the *Tao Te Ching*; for example, the 'gods in the valley' are identical with the 'valley-spirit' of Lao-tse. But while Taoism degenerated more and more in the Han[2] period into an external wizardry, owing to the fact that the Taoist court magicians were seeking to find by alchemy the golden pill (the philosopher's stone), which would create gold out of the baser metals and lend men physical immortality, Lü Yen's movement represented a reform. The alchemistic signs became symbols of psychological processes. In this respect there was a close approach to the original ideas of Lao-tse. The latter, however, was altogether a free spirit, and his follower, Chuàng-tzu, scorned all the hocus-pocus of yoga practice, nature-healers, and seekers after the elixir of life, although he himself, of course, also practised

[1] In the year 1891, 15,000 members were killed by Manchu hirelings.
[2] Third century B.C. to third century A.D. (C. F. B.)

6

meditation and by means of it attained that intuition of unity upon which was founded his later, intellectually developed system. In Lü Yen there was a certain faith, a religious trend, which, stimulated by Buddhism, convinced him of the illusory quality of all external things, but in a way clearly different from Buddhism. He seeks, with all his might, the fixed pole in the flight of phenomena, where the adept can attain eternal life, a thought absolutely foreign to Buddhism, which denies any substance to the ego. Nevertheless, the influence of Mahayana Buddhism, which at that time dominated thought in China, is not to be underrated. Buddhist sutras are cited time and again. In our text, indeed, this influence is even greater than can be assumed to have been the case in the *Chin-tan-chiao* (Religion of the Golden Elixir of Life) in general. In the second half of the third section, explicit reference is made to the method known as 'fixating contemplation' (*chih-kuan*), and the latter is a purely Buddhist method which was practised in the *T'ien-t'ai* School of Chih K'ai [Chih I, A.D. 531-597].

From this point on, a certain break in the sequence of thought in our essay becomes noticeable. On the one hand, the cultivation of the Golden Flower is further described; on the other hand, there appear purely Buddhist ideas which repudiate the world and emphatically shift the goal towards nirvana. Then follow several sections[1] which, considering the spiritual elevation and coherence of the work as a whole, have scarcely more value than gleanings. Moreover, the work towards an inner rebirth through the 'circulation of the light', and the creation of the divine seed-kernel, is described only in its first stages, although the later stages are named as the goal. (Compare the *Hui Ming Ching* of Liu Hua-yang, where these later stages are more carefully explained.) Therefore, we cannot escape the suspicion that a portion of the manuscript has actually been lost, and substitutions made from other sources. If that is so,

[1] These sections are omitted from the present translation. (R. W.)

7

it would explain the break in continuity and the inferior quality of the parts not translated here.

An unprejudiced reading will, however, disclose the fact that these two sources, Taoism and Buddhism, do not suffice to cover the whole range of thought: Confucianism in the form which is based on the *I Ching* is also introduced. The eight basic trigrams (*Pa Kua*) of the *I Ching* are brought into various passages of our text as symbols for certain inner processes, and further on we shall try to explain the influence resulting from this use of the symbols. For the rest, since Confucianism has a broad common base with Taoism, the union of these two schools of thought did not bring about a loss in coherence.

Perhaps it will strike many a European reader as remarkable that there appear in the text sayings familiar to him from Christian teaching, while, on the other hand, these same well-known things which in Europe are very often taken only as ecclesiastical phrasing are here given quite a different perspective, because of the psychological connections in which they are used. We find intuitions and concepts like the following, to select only at random a few that are especially striking: Light is the life of man. The eye is the light of the body. Man is spiritually reborn out of water and fire, to which must be added 'thought-earth' (spirit), as womb, or tilled field. Let us compare the sayings of John: 'I baptize you with water: after me shall come one who will baptize with the Holy Ghost and with fire'; or: 'Except a man be born of water and of the spirit, he cannot enter into the kingdom of God.' How suggestive, for instance, becomes the thought of 'water' as the seed-substance in our text, and how clear the difference between the 'outward-streaming' activity which exhausts itself in begetting (what is born of flesh remains flesh), and the 'backward-flowing' movement (*metanoia*).

The bath, too, plays its part in this rebirth just as it does in the baptism preached by John and also in the Christian baptism.

Even the mystical marriage, which plays such an important rôle in Christian parables, appears several times; there is also mentioned the child, the boy within ourselves (the *puer aeternus*, the Christ, who must be born in us and who, in another way, is the bridegroom of the soul), and the bride as well. And what is most striking of all, perhaps, even an apparently minor detail, the need of having oil in the lamps so that they can burn brightly, takes on a new and weighty psychological meaning in our text. It is worth mentioning that the expression 'Golden Flower' (*Chin Hua*), in an esoteric connection, includes the word 'light'. If one writes the two characters one above the other, so that they touch, the lower part of the upper character and the upper part of the lower character make the character for 'light' (*kuang*). Obviously this secret sign was invented in a time of persecution, when a veil of deep secrecy was necessary to the further promulgation of the doctrine. That was in turn the reason the teaching always remained limited to secret circles. Even to-day, however, its membership is greater than appears from the outside.

If we ask whence this light-religion comes, we can first of all consider Persia, as in the T'ang period there were Persian temples in many places in China. But even though certain points correspond with the religion of Zarathustra, and especially with Persian mysticism, there are, on the other hand, very strong divergences. Another view to be considered is that of a direct Christian influence. In the T'ang period the religion of a Turkic tribe, the Uigurs, who were allied with the Emperor, was the Nestorian branch of Christianity; it stood in high favour, as is witnessed by the well-known Nestorian monument in Sianfu erected in 781, and bearing both a Chinese and a Syriac inscription. Thus connections between the Nestorians and the *Chin-tan-chiao* are quite possible. Timothy Richard went so far as to consider the *Chin-tan-chiao* simply a survival of the old Nestorians. He was led to his view by certain agreements in ritual and certain traditions of the *Chin-tan-chiao* membership which approach closely to Christian practice. Lately P. Y. Saeki[1] has taken up the theory again and, supported by the Nestorian liturgy found in Tun-huang by Pelliot, has established a series of further parallels. He even goes so far as to identify Lü Yen, the founder of the *Chin-tan-chiao*, with the Adam who wrote the text of the Nestorian monument and signs himself with the Chinese name Lü Hsiu-yen. According to this hypothesis, Lü Yen, the founder of the *Chin-tan-chiao*, would have been a Christian of the Nestorian confession! Saeki goes decidedly too far in his delight in identifications: his proofs are all of them almost convincing, but there is always lacking the crucial point which would clinch the matter. Many partial proofs do not make a whole one, but we must concur with him at least to the extent of agreeing that in the *Chin-tan-chiao* there has been a strong admixture of Nestorian ideas which are also evident in the present manuscript. Some of these ideas seem very odd in their strange dress, while others take on a remarkable, new sort of vitality. Here we reach one of those points which prove over and over again:

> *Orient und Occident*
> *Sind nicht mehr zu trennen.*[2]

2. The Psychological and Cosmological Premises of the Text

To make the following translation intelligible, it is worth while to say a few more words about the foundations of the philosophy on which the method rests. This philosophy is, to a certain extent, the common property of all Chinese philoso-

---

[1] *The Nestorian Monument in China*, London, 2nd edition, 1928.
[2] 'East and West
Can no longer be kept apart.' (Goethe)

phical trends. It is built on the premise that the cosmos and man, in the last analysis, obey the same law; that man is a microcosm and is not separated from the macrocosm by any fixed barriers. The very same laws rule for the one as for the other, and from the one a way leads into the other. The psyche and the cosmos are to each other like the inner world and the outer world. Therefore man participates by nature in all cosmic events, and is inwardly as well as outwardly interwoven with them.

The Tao, then, the Way, governs man just as it does invisible and visible nature (heaven and earth). The character for Tao in its original form[1] consists of a head, which probably must be interpreted as 'beginning', and then the character for 'going' in its dual form in which it also means 'track', and underneath, the character for 'standing still', which is omitted in the later way of writing. The original meaning, then, is that of a 'track which, though fixed itself, leads from a beginning directly to the goal'. The fundamental idea is that the Tao, though itself motionless, is the means of all movement and gives it law. Heavenly paths are those along which the constellations move; the path of man is the way along which he must travel. Lao-tse has used this word, though in the metaphysical sense, as the final world principle, which antedates realization and is not yet divided by the drawing apart of the opposites on which emergence into reality depends. This terminology is presupposed in the present book.

In Confucianism there is a certain difference in terminology. There the word 'Tao' has an inner-world significance and means the 'right way'; on the one hand, the way of heaven, on the other, the way of man. To Confucianism, the final principle of an undivided One is the *T'ai-chi* (the great ridge-pole, the supreme ultimate). The term 'pole' occa-

[1] Compare *Ku-chou-pien*, vol. 66, pp. 25ff., which was also consulted with respect to the analysis of the other characters.

sionally appears in our text also, and is there identical with Tao.

Out of the Tao, and the *T'ai-chi*, there develop the principles of reality, the one pole being the light (yang) and the other the dark, or the shadowy (yin). Among European scholars, some have turned first to sexual references for an explanation, but the characters refer to phenomena in nature. Yin is shade, therefore the north side of a mountain and the south side of a river (because during the day the position of the sun makes the south side of the river appear dark). Yang, in its original form, indicates flying pennants and, corresponding to the character yin, is the south side of a mountain and the north side of a river. Starting only with the meaning of 'light' and 'dark', the principle was then expanded to all polar opposites, including the sexual. However, since both yin and yang have their common origin in an undivided One and are active only in the realm of phenomena, where yang appears as the active principle and conditions, and yin as the passive principle is derived and conditioned, it is quite clear that a metaphysical dualism is not the basis of these ideas. Less abstract than yin and yang are the concepts of the Creative and the Receptive (*Ch'ien* and *K'un*) that originate in the *Book of Changes* [*I Ching*], and are symbolized by heaven and earth. Through the union of heaven and earth, and through the efficacy of the dual primal forces within this field of activity (governed by the one primal law, the Tao), there develop the 'ten thousand things', that is, the outer world.

Among these things, viewed externally, is also to be found man in his corporeal appearance, which, in all its parts, is a small universe (*hsiao t'ien-ti*). So, according to the Confucians, the inner nature of man comes from heaven, or, as the Taoists express it, it is a phenomenal form of the Tao. In the phenomenal world man develops into a multiplicity of individuals in each of whom the central monad is enclosed as the life-principle; but immediately, before birth even, at the moment of conception, it separates into the bi-polar phenomena of human nature and life (*hsing* and *ming*). The word for human nature (*hsing*) is made up of those for heart or mind (*hsin*), and origin, being born (*sheng*). The heart (*hsin*), according to the Chinese idea, is the seat of emotional consciousness, which is awakened by the five senses through unreflecting reactions to impressions received from the external world. That which remains as a substratum when no feelings are being expressed, but which lingers, so to speak, in a transcendental, supra-conscious condition, is human nature (*hsing*). Varying according to the more exact definition of this concept, human nature is either originally good, if looked at from the standpoint of the eternal idea (Mencius), or it is originally evil, or at best neutral. Taken from the standpoint of empirical-historical evolution, it can be made into something good only by a long development of the mores (Hsün Ch'ing).

Human nature (*hsing*), as an idea undoubtedly related to logos, appears closely knit with life (*ming*) when entering the phenomenal world. The character *ming* really signifies a royal command, then destiny, fate, the fate allotted to a man, so too, the duration of the life-span, the measure of vital energy at one's disposal, and thus it comes about that *ming* (life) is closely related to eros. Both principles are, so to speak, supra-individual. Man as a spiritual being is made human by his nature (*hsing*). The individual man possesses it, but it extends far beyond the limits of the individual. Life (*ming*) is also supra-individual in that man must simply accept his destiny; it does not stem from his conscious will. Confucianism sees in *ming*, life, a heaven-made law to which man must adapt; Taoism takes it as the multi-coloured play of nature which cannot evade the laws of the Tao, but which is yet pure coincidence; Chinese Buddhism sees it as the working out of karma within the world of illusion.

To these dualities there correspond in the corporeal-personal man the following bi-polar tensions. The body is activated by the interplay of two psychic structures: first, *hun*, which, because it belongs to the yang principle, I have translated as animus,[1] and secondly, *p'o*, which belongs to the yin principle, and is rendered by me as anima.[2] Both ideas come from observation of what takes place at death, and therefore both contain in their written form the sign for demon,[3] that is, the departed one (*kuei*). The anima was thought of as especially linked with the bodily processes; at death it sinks to the earth and decays. The animus, on the other hand, is the higher soul; after death it rises in the air, where at first it is still active for a time and then evaporates in ethereal space, or flows back into the common reservoir of life. In living men, the two correspond in a certain degree to the cerebral system and the system of the solar plexus respectively. The animus dwells in the eyes, the anima in the abdomen. The animus is bright and active, the anima is dark and earth-bound. The sign for *hun* (animus) is made up of the characters for 'demon' and 'cloud', while

[1] Wilhelm's use of the term 'animus' lends the latter a meaning quite different from that given it by Jung's concept, where the animus is an element in a woman's mind. Jung finds *hun* close to the meaning of logos, but the latter term could not be used for *hun*, first, because of there being another Chinese concept still closer to logos, i.e. *hsing* (human nature), and also because *hun* is described as being a personal factor, while logos is strictly impersonal. The expression 'spirit-soul' as opposed to 'earthly soul', *p'o*, would seem to cover the meaning of *hun* as explained by Wilhelm, and in order to avoid a possible confusion in terminology it was planned to make this alteration in the English version, the authors having agreed that a change was advisable. But though the proposed substitution would undoubtedly simplify things for the reader and would involve no change in meaning, still it would require the rearrangement of several paragraphs and thus cause too great a divergence between the two editions. For that reason, the change has not been made. (C. F. B.)

[2] It is to be noted that *p'o* corresponds to only one part of the anima as conceived by Jung. In the latter's concept, the spiritual side of the anima is quite as important as the animal side. (C. F. B.)

[3] The word for 'demon' in Chinese does not necessarily have an evil connotation. (C. F. B.)

that for *p'o* (anima) is composed of the characters for 'demon' and 'white'. This would indicate ideas similar to what we find appearing elsewhere as shadow-soul and body-soul, and without a doubt the Chinese concept is meant to include something like this. None the less, we must be cautious in the matter of derivations, because in the most ancient script the graph for demon is lacking and so we may perhaps be dealing with primary, not derived, symbols. In any case, animus (*hun*) is the light, yang-soul, while anima (*p'o*) is the dark, yin-soul.

The usual, 'clockwise-flowing',[1] that is, the downward-flowing life-process, is the one in which the two souls enter into relations as the intellectual and animal factors. As a rule, it will be the anima, the undiscriminating will, which, goaded by passions, forces the animus or intellect into its service. At least the anima will do this to the extent that the intellect directs itself outward, whereby the energies of both animus and anima leak away and life consumes itself. A positive result is the creation of new beings in which life continues, while the original being 'externalizes' itself and 'ultimately is made by things into a thing'. The result is death. The anima sinks, the animus rises, and the ego, robbed of its energy, is left behind in a dubious condition.

---

[1] The German word used is *rechtläufig*, which, translated literally, means 'right-flowing'. In the text it describes 'energies' in the body which flow downward, and so in all instances except the above it has been translated as downward-flowing. When the energies in the body are not allowed to go their natural, downward course, but are dammed up, the movement is described as backward-flowing (*rückläufig*). The yoga system teaches a technique of meditation whereby the natural flow of energy can be reversed, and the energy made to rise to the higher centres, where it becomes spirit. Leaving out this end result, it is easy for the student of analytical psychology to see a connection between the two streams of energy and the concepts of extraversion and introversion. An important difference is that extraversion and introversion apply only to the movement of psychic energy, whereas the Chinese concept seems to include both psychic and physiological processes. (C. F. B.)

If the ego has acquiesced in the 'externalization', it follows the downward pull and sinks into the dull misery of death, only poorly nourished by the illusory images of life by which it is still attracted without being able to participate in anything actively (hells, hungry souls). But if the ego has made an effort to strive upward in spite of the process of 'externalization', it maintains for a time (as long, in fact, as it is reinforced by the energies expressed in sacrifices by the survivors) a relatively happy life, each according to its deserts. In both cases, the personal element retreats and there ensues an involution corresponding to the 'externalization'. The being then becomes an impotent phantom because it lacks the energies of life and its fate comes to an end. It now partakes of the fruits of its good or bad deeds in heavens or hells, which, however, are not external, but purely inner states. The more a being penetrates these states, the more involution progresses till finally he disappears from the plane of existence, of whatever nature that may have been, and then, by entering a new womb, begins a new existence supplied by his previous imaginings. This condition is the state of the demon, the spirit, the departed one, the one who withdraws. The Chinese word for this state of being is *kuei* (often wrongly translated by 'devil').

If, on the other hand, it has been possible during life to set going the 'backward-flowing', rising movement of the life-energies, if the energies of the anima are mastered by the animus, then a liberation from external things takes place. They are recognized but not desired. Thus illusion is robbed of its energy. An inner, ascending circulation of the energies takes place. The ego withdraws from its entanglement in the world, and after death remains alive because 'interiorization' has prevented the wasting of the life-energies in the outer world. Instead of these being dissipated they have created within the inner rotation of the monad a life-centre which is independent of bodily existence. Such an ego is a god, *deus, shen*. The character for *shen* means to extend, to create; in a word, it is the opposite of *kuei*. In the oldest Chinese script it is represented by a double meander pattern, which can also mean thunder, lightning, electrical stimulation. Such a being survives as long as the inner rotation continues. It can, even though invisible, still influence men and inspire them to great thoughts and noble deeds. The saints and sages of ancient times are beings like these, who for thousands of years have stimulated and educated humanity.

However, there remains one limitation. These beings retain a personal character, and are therefore subject to the effects of space and time. Neither are they immortal any more than heaven and earth are eternal. The Golden Flower alone, which grows out of inner detachment from all entanglement with things, is eternal. A man who reaches this stage transposes his ego; he is no longer limited to the monad, but penetrates the magic circle of the polar duality of all phenomena and returns to the undivided One, the Tao. Herein lies a difference between Buddhism and Taoism. In Buddhism this return to nirvana is connected with a complete extinction of the ego, which, like the world, is only illusion. If nirvana may not be explained as death, cessation, still it is strictly transcendent. In Taoism, on the other hand, the goal is to preserve in a transfigured form the idea of the person, the 'traces' left by experience. That is the light which, with life, returns to itself and which is symbolized in our text by the Golden Flower.

As a supplement, we must still add a few words about the use in our text of the eight trigrams of the *Book of Changes* (*I Ching*). The trigram *Chen* ☳, thunder, the Arousing, is life which breaks out of the depths of the earth; it is the beginning of all movement. The trigram *Sun* ☴, wind, wood, the Gentle, characterizes the streaming of the reality-energies into the form of the idea. Just as wind pervades all places, so the principle for which *Sun* stands is all-penetrating, and creates 'realization'. The trigram *Li* ⚌ ⚍, sun, fire, the lucid, the Clinging, plays a great rôle in this religion of light. It dwells in the eyes, forms the protecting circle, and brings about rebirth. The trigram *K'un* ⚏ ⚏, earth, the Receptive, is one of the two primal principles, namely the yin principle which is embodied in the energies of the earth. It is the earth which, as a tilled field, takes up the seed of heaven and gives it form. The trigram *Tui* ⚌ ⚊, lake, mist, the Joyous, is a final condition on the yin side, and therefore belongs to autumn. The trigram *Ch'ien* ☰, heaven, the Creative, the strong, is the embodiment of the yang principle which fertilizes *K'un*, the Receptive. The trigram *K'an* ⚍ ⚍, water, the Abysmal, is the opposite of *Li* ⚌ ⚍, as is already shown in its outer structure. It represents the region of eros, while *Li* stands for logos. *Li* is the sun, *K'an* the moon. The marriage of *K'an* and *Li* is the secret magical process which produces the child, the new man. The trigram *Ken* ⚍ ⚏, mountain, Keeping Still, is the symbol of meditation, which, by keeping external things quiescent, gives life to the inner world. Therefore *Ken* is the place where death and life meet, where '*Stirb und Werde*' is consummated.

TRANSLATION

OF THE

T'AI I CHIN HUA TSUNG CHIH

I. HEAVENLY CONSCIOUSNESS (THE HEART)

Master Lü-tsu said, That which exists through itself is called the Way (Tao). Tao has neither name nor shape. It is the one essence,[1] the one primal spirit. Essence and life cannot be seen. They are contained in the light of heaven. The light of heaven cannot be seen. It is contained in the two eyes. To-day I will be your guide and will first reveal to you the secret of the Golden Flower of the great One, and, starting from that, I will explain the rest in detail.

The great One is the term given to that which has nothing above it. The secret of the magic of life consists in using action in order to attain non-action. One must not wish to leap over everything and penetrate directly. The maxim handed down to us is to take in hand the work on human nature (*hsing*). In doing this it is important not to take any wrong path.

The Golden Flower is the light. What colour is the light? One uses the Golden Flower as a symbol. It is the true energy of the transcendent great One. The phrase 'The lead of the water-region has but one taste' refers to it.

Heaven created water through the One.[2] That is the true energy of the great One. If man attains this One he becomes alive; if he loses it he dies. But even if man lives in the energy (vital breath, *prana*) he does not see the energy (vital breath), just as fishes live in water but do not see the water. Man dies when he has no vital breath, just as fishes perish when deprived of water. Therefore the adepts have taught people to hold fast to the primal, and to guard

[1] *Hsing*, otherwise translated as 'human nature'. (C. F. B.)
[2] In the German text the *Book of Changes* is said to be the origin of this sentence. It does not occur there, and so, with the permission of Hellmut Wilhelm, the statement has been omitted.

21

the One; it is the circulation of the light and the maintaining of the centre. If one guards this true energy, one can prolong the span of life, and can then apply the method of creating an immortal body by 'melting and mixing'.[1]

The work on the circulation of the light depends entirely on the backward-flowing movement, so that the thoughts (the place of heavenly consciousness, the heavenly heart) are gathered together. The heavenly heart lies between sun and moon (i.e. between the two eyes).

The *Book of the Yellow Castle* says: 'In the square inch field of the square foot house, life can be regulated.' The square foot house is the face. The square inch field in the face: what could that be other than the heavenly heart? In the middle of the square inch dwells the splendour. In the purple hall of the city of jade dwells the God of Utmost Emptiness and Life. The Confucians call it the centre of emptiness; the Buddhists, the terrace of living; the Taoists, the ancestral land, or the yellow castle, or the dark pass, or the space of former heaven. The heavenly heart is like the dwelling place, the light is the master.

Therefore when the light circulates, the energies of the whole body appear before its throne, as, when a holy king has established the capital and has laid down the fundamental rules of order, all the states approach with tribute; or as, when the master is quiet and calm, men-servants and maids obey his orders of their own accord, and each does his work.

Therefore you only have to make the light circulate: that is the deepest and most wonderful secret. The light is easy to move, but difficult to fix. If it is made to circulate long enough, then it crystallizes itself; that is the natural spirit-body. This crystallized spirit is formed beyond the nine heavens. It is the

---

[1] This commentary probably comes from the seventeenth or eighteenth century. (The footnotes arranged by Wilhelm have been placed with the text. In the previous edition, in agreement with the German, they followed the text. C. F. B.)

condition of which it is said in the *Book of the Seal of the Heart*: 'Silently thou fliest upward in the morning.'

In carrying out this fundamental principle you need to seek for no other methods, but must only concentrate your thoughts on it. The book *Leng Yen*[1] says: 'By collecting the thoughts one can fly and will be born in heaven.' Heaven is not the wide blue sky but the place where corporeality is begotten in the house of the Creative. If one keeps this up for a long time there develops quite naturally, in addition to the body, yet another spirit-body.

The Golden Flower is the Elixir of Life (*Chin-tan*; literally, golden ball, golden pill). All changes of spiritual consciousness depend upon the heart. There is a secret charm which, although it works very accurately, is yet so fluid that it needs extreme intelligence and clarity, and the most complete absorption and tranquillity. People without this highest degree of intelligence and understanding do not find the way to apply the charm; people without this utmost capacity for absorption and tranquillity cannot keep fast hold of it.

This section explains the origin of the great Way (the Tao) of the world. The heavenly heart is the germ of the great Way. If you can be absolutely quiet then the heavenly heart will spontaneously manifest itself. When the feeling stirs and expresses itself in the normal flow, man is created as primal creature. This creature abides between conception and birth in true space; when the one note of individuation enters into the birth, human nature and life are divided in two. From this time on, if the utmost quietness is not achieved, human nature and life never see each other again.

Therefore it is said in the Plan of the Supreme Ultimate[2] that the great One includes within itself true energy (prana), seed, spirit, animus, and anima. If the thoughts are absolutely tranquil so that the heavenly heart can be seen, the spiritual intelligence reaches the

---

[1] *Leng Yen* is the Buddhist *Suramgama Sutra*.

[2] See Chung-yuan Chang's essay, *Self Realization and the Inner Process of Peace*, in the *Eranos Jahrbuch*, Zürich, 1956. (C. F. B.)

origin unaided. This human nature lives indeed in true space, but the radiance of the light dwells in the two eyes. Therefore the Master teaches the circulation of the light so that the true human nature may be reached. The true human nature is the primal spirit. The primal spirit is precisely human nature and life, and if one accepts what is real in it, it is the primal energy. And the great Way is just this thing.

The Master is further concerned that people should not miss the way that leads from conscious action to unconscious non-action. Therefore he says, the magic of the Elixir of Life makes use of conscious action in order that unconscious non-action may be attained. Conscious action consists in setting the light in circulation by reflection in order to make manifest the release of heaven. If then the true seed is born, and the right method applied in order to melt and mix it, and in that way to create the Elixir of Life, then one goes through the pass. The embryo, which must be developed by the work of warming, nourishing, bathing, and washing, is formed. That passes over into the realm of unconscious non-action. A whole year of this fire-period is needed before the embryo is born, sheds the shells, and passes out of the ordinary world into the holy world.

This method is quite simple and easy. But there are so many transforming and changing conditions connected with it that it is said that not with one leap can a man suddenly get there. Whoever seeks eternal life must search for the place whence human nature and life originally sprang.

2. The Primal Spirit and the Conscious Spirit

Master Lü-tsu said, In comparison with heaven and earth, man is like a mayfly. But compared to the great Way, heaven and earth, too, are like a bubble and a shadow. Only the primal spirit and the true nature overcome time and space.

The energy of the seed, like heaven and earth, is transitory, but the primal spirit is beyond the polar differences. Here is the place whence heaven and earth derive their being. When students understand how to grasp the primal spirit they overcome the polar opposites of light and darkness and tarry no longer in the three worlds.[1] But only he who has envisioned human nature's original face is able to do this.

When men are set free from the womb, the primal spirit dwells in the square inch (between the eyes), but the conscious spirit dwells below in the heart. This lower fleshly heart has the shape of a large peach: it is covered by the wings of the lungs, supported by the liver, and served by the bowels. This heart is dependent on the outside world. If a man does not eat for one day even, it feels extremely uncomfortable. If it hears something terrifying it throbs; if it hears something enraging it stops; if it is faced with death it becomes sad; if it sees something beautiful it is dazzled. But the heavenly heart in the head, when would it have moved in the least? Dost thou ask: Can the heavenly heart not move? Then I answer: How could the true thought in the square inch move! If it really moves, that is not good. For when ordinary men die, then it moves, but that is not good. It is best indeed if the light has already solidified into a spirit-body and its life-energy gradually penetrated the instincts and movements. But that is a secret which has not been revealed for thousands of years.

The lower heart moves like a strong, powerful commander who despises the heavenly ruler because of his weakness, and has usurped the leadership in affairs of state. But when the primal castle can be fortified and defended, then it is as if a strong and wise ruler sat upon the throne. The eyes start the light circulating like two ministers at the right and left who support the ruler with all their might. When rule in the centre is thus in order, all those rebellious heroes will present themselves with lances reversed ready to take orders.

The way to the Elixir of Life knows as supreme magic, seed-water, spirit-fire, and thought-earth: these three. What is seed-water? It is the true, one energy of former heaven (eros).

---

[1] Heaven, earth, hell.

Spirit-fire is the light (logos). Thought-earth is the heavenly heart of the middle dwelling (intuition). Spirit-fire is used for effecting, thought-earth for substance, and seed-water for the foundation. Ordinary men make their bodies through thoughts. The body is not only the seven-foot-tall outer body. In the body is the anima. The anima adheres to consciousness, in order to affect it. Consciousness depends for its origin on the anima. The anima is feminine (yin), it is the substance of consciousness. As long as this consciousness is not interrupted, it continues to beget from generation to generation, and the changes of form of the anima and the transformations of substance are unceasing.

But, besides this, there is the animus in which the spirit shelters. The animus lives in the daytime in the eyes; at night it houses in the liver. When living in the eyes, it sees; when housed in the liver, it dreams. Dreams are the wanderings of the spirit through all nine heavens and all nine earths. But whoever is in a dark and withdrawn mood on waking, and chained to his bodily form, is fettered by the anima. Therefore the concentration of the animus is brought about by the circulation of the light, and in this way the spirit is maintained, the anima subjugated, and consciousness cut off. The method used by the ancients for escaping from the world consisted in melting out completely the slag of darkness in order to return to the purely creative. This is nothing more than a reduction of the anima and a completion of the animus. And the circulation of the light is the magical means of reducing the dark, and gaining mastery over the anima. Even if the work is not directed towards bringing back the Creative, but confines itself to the magical means of the circulation of the light, it is just the light that is the Creative. By means of its circulation, one returns to the Creative. If this method is followed, plenty of seed-water will be present of itself; the spirit-fire will be ignited, and the thought-earth will solidify and crystallize. And thus the holy fruit matures. The scarabaeus rolls his ball

坐禪圖

凝神入氣穴
孔子之謂心
老子之謂竅
釋之謂止此

坐久忽所知忽覺月在地
冷冷天風來驀然到肝肺
俯視一泓水澄湛無物蔽
中有蟄逸黙黙自相契

無事此靜坐一日如兩日
若活七十年便是百四十
靜坐少思寡欲真心養氣存神
此是偸真要訣學者可以青邨

Meditation, Stage 1: Gathering the light.

and in the ball there develops life as the result of the undivided effort of his spiritual concentration. If now an embryo can grow in manure, and shed its shells, why should not the dwelling place of our heavenly heart also be able to create a body if we concentrate the spirit upon it?

The one effective, true human nature (logos united with vitality), when it descends into the house of the Creative, divides into animus and anima. The animus is in the heavenly heart. It is of the nature of light; it is the power of lightness and purity. It is that which we have received from the great emptiness, that which is identical in form with the primordial beginning. The anima partakes of the nature of the dark. It is the energy of the heavy and the turbid; it is bound to the bodily fleshly heart. The animus loves life. The anima seeks death. All sensuous desires and impulses of anger are effects of the anima; it is the conscious spirit which after death is nourished on blood, but which, during life, is in greatest distress. The dark returns to darkness and like things attract each other according to their kind. But the pupil understands how to distil the dark anima completely so that it transforms itself into pure light (*yang*).[1]

In this part there is described the rôle played by the primal spirit and the conscious spirit in the making of the human body. The Master says, The life of man is like that of a mayfly: only the true human nature of the primal spirit can transcend the cycle of heaven and earth and the fate of the aeons. The true human nature proceeds from that which has no polarity [the ultimateless] and receives the primal energy of polarity [the ultimate] whereby it takes the true essence of heaven and earth into itself and becomes the conscious spirit. As primal spirit it receives its human nature from father and mother. This primal spirit is without consciousness and knowledge, but is able to regulate the formative processes of the body. The conscious spirit is very evident and very effective, and can adapt itself unceasingly. It is the ruler of the human heart. As

---

[1] Light is meant here as a world principle, the positive pole, not as light that shines.

long as it stays in the body it is the animus. After its departure from the body it becomes spirit. While the body is entering into existence, the primal spirit has not yet formed an embryo in which it could incorporate itself. Thus it crystallizes itself in the non-polarized free One.

At the time of birth the conscious spirit inhales the energy and thus becomes the dwelling of the new-born. It lives in the heart. From that time on the heart is master, and the primal spirit loses its place while the conscious spirit has the power.

The primal spirit loves stillness, and the conscious spirit loves movement. In its movement it remains bound to feelings and desires. Day and night it wastes the primal seed till the energy of the primal spirit is entirely used up. Then the conscious spirit leaves the shell and goes away.

Whoever has done good in the main has spirit-energy that is pure and clear when death comes. It passes out by the upper openings of mouth and nose. The pure and light energy rises upward and floats up to heaven and becomes the fivefold present shadow-genius, or shadow-spirit. But if, during life, the primal spirit was used by the conscious spirit for avarice, folly, desire, and lust, and committed all sorts of sins, then in the moment of death the spirit-energy is turbid and confused, and the conscious spirit passes out together with the breath, through the lower openings of the door of the belly. For if the spirit-energy is turbid and unclean, it crystallizes downward, sinks down to hell, and becomes a demon. Then not only does the primal spirit lose its nature, but the power and wisdom of true human nature is thereby lessened. Therefore the Master says, If it moves, that is not good.

If one wants to maintain the primal spirit one must, without fail, first subjugate the perceiving spirit. The way to subjugate it is through the circulation of the light. If one practises the circulation of the light, one must forget both body and heart. The heart must die, the spirit live. When the spirit lives, the breath will begin to circulate in a wonderful way. This is what the Master called the very best.[1] Then the spirit must be allowed to dive down into the

---

[1] The four stages of rebirth are characterized here. Rebirth (out of water and spirit) is the development of the pneumatic body within the perishable body of the flesh. In this there is apparent a relationship to the thought of Paul and John.

abdomen (solar plexus). The energy then has intercourse with spirit, and spirit unites with the energy and crystallizes itself. This is the method of starting the work.

In time, the primal spirit transforms itself in the dwelling of life into the true energy. At that time, the method of the turning of the millwheel must be applied, in order to distil it so that it becomes the Elixir of Life. That is the method of concentrated work.

When the Life Elixir pearl is finished, the holy embryo can be formed; then the work must be directed to the warming and nourishing of the spiritual embryo. That is the method of finishing.

When the energy-body of the child is fully formed, the work must be so directed that the embryo is born and returns to emptiness. That is the method of ending the work.

From the most ancient times till to-day, this is not empty talk, but the sequence of the great Way in the true method of producing an eternally living and immortal spirit and holy man.

But if the work is so far consummated, then everything belonging to the dark principle is wholly absorbed, and the body is born into pure light. When the conscious spirit has been transformed into the primal spirit, then only can one say that it has attained an infinite capacity for transformation and, departing from the cycle of births, has been brought to the sixfold[1] present, golden genius. If this method of ennobling is not applied, how will the way of being born and dying be escaped?

3. CIRCULATION OF THE LIGHT AND PROTECTION OF THE CENTRE

Master Lü-tsu said, Since when has the expression 'circulation of the light' been revealed? It was revealed by the 'True Men of the Beginning of Form' (Kuan Yin-hsi).[2] When the light is made to move in a circle, all the energies of heaven and earth, of the light and the dark, are crystallized. That is what is

[1] The fivefold present spirit into which the man who has striven towards the good, but blindly, is transformed at his death, is limited to the region of the five senses, and is therefore still imprisoned on this earth. Rebirth effects his transition into the sixth, the spiritual, realm.

[2] A pupil of Lao-tse. (According to legend. H. W.)

termed seed-like thinking, or purification of the energy, or purification of the idea. When one begins to apply this magic it is as if, in the middle of being, there were non-being. When in the course of time the work is completed, and beyond the body there is a body, it is as if, in the middle of non-being, there were being. Only after concentrated work of a hundred days will the light be genuine, then only will it become spirit-fire. After a hundred days there develops by itself in the midst of the light a point of the true light-pole (yang). Then suddenly there develops the seed pearl. It is as if man and woman embraced and a conception took place. Then one must be quite still and wait. The circulation of the light is the epoch of fire.

In the midst of primal transformation, the radiance of the light (*yang-kuang*) is the determining thing. In the physical world it is the sun; in man, the eye. The radiation and dissipation of spiritual consciousness is chiefly brought about by this energy when it is directed outward (flows downward). Therefore the Way of the Golden Flower depends wholly on the backward-flowing method.

Man's heart stands under the fire sign.[1] The flames of the fire press upward. When both eyes are looking at things of the world it is with vision directed outward. Now if one closes the eyes and, reversing the glance, directs it inward and looks at the room of the ancestors, that is the backward-flowing method. The energy of the kidneys is under the water sign. When the desires are stirred, it runs downward, is directed outward, and creates children. If, in the moment of release, it is not allowed to flow outward, but is led

---

[1] The two psychic poles are here contrasted with one another. They are represented as logos (heart, consciousness), to be found under the fire trigram [*Li*], and eros (kidneys, sexuality), under the water trigram [*K'an*]. The 'natural' man lets both these energies work outwardly (intellect and the process of procreation); thus, they 'stream out' and are consumed. The adept turns them inward and brings them together, whereby they fertilize one another and produce a psychically vital, and therefore strong, life of the spirit.

back by the energy of thought so that it penetrates the crucible of the Creative, and refreshes heart and body and nourishes them, that also is the backward-flowing method. Therefore it is said, The Way of the Elixir of Life depends entirely on the backward-flowing method.

The circulation of the light is not only a circulation of the seed-blossom of the individual body, but it is even a circulation of the true, creative, formative energies. It is not a momentary fantasy, but the exhaustion of the cycle (soul-migrations) of all the aeons. Therefore the duration of a breath means a year according to human reckoning and a hundred years measured by the long night of the nine paths (of reincarnations).

After a man has the one sound of individuation[1] behind him, he will be born outward according to the circumstances, and until his old age he will never look backward. The energy of the light exhausts itself and trickles away. That brings the ninefold darkness (of reincarnations) into the world. In the book *Leng Yen*[2] it is said: 'By concentrating the thoughts, one can fly; by concentrating the desires, one falls.' When a pupil takes little care of his thoughts and much care of his desires, he gets into the path of submersion. Only through contemplation and quietness does true intuition arise: for that the backward-flowing method is necessary.

In the *Book of the Secret Correspondences*[3] it is said: 'Release

[1] The character 'ho' translated here by 'individuation' is written with the symbol for 'energy' inside an 'enclosure'. Thus it means the form of the entelechy imprinted in the monad. It is the detaching of a unit of energy and the enveloping of it with seed-energies that lead to embodiment. The process is conceived of as connected with a sound. Empirically it coincides with conception. From that time on, there takes place an ever-advancing 'development', 'unfolding', until birth brings the individual to light. From then on it automatically continues further till the energy is exhausted and death ensues.

[2] The *Suramgama Sutra*, a Buddhist sutra.

[3] *Yin fu-ching*, a Taoist classic. (For an English translation see Frederick Henry Balfour, *Taoist Texts*, London and Shanghai, n.d., pp. 49–62. H. W.)

is in the eye.' In the *Simple Questions of the Yellow Ruler*[1] it is said: 'The seed-blossoms of the human body must be concentrated upward in the empty space.' This refers to it. Immortality is contained in this sentence and also the overcoming of the world is contained in it. This is the common goal of all religions.

The light is not in the body alone, nor is it only outside the body. Mountains and rivers and the great earth are lit by sun and moon; all that is this light. Therefore it is not only within the body. Understanding and clarity, perception and enlightenment, and all movements (of the spirit) are likewise this light; therefore it is not just something outside the body. The light-flower of heaven and earth fills all the thousand spaces. But also the light-flower of the individual body passes through heaven and covers the earth. Therefore, as soon as the light is circulating, heaven and earth, mountains and rivers, are all circulating with it at the same time. To concentrate the seed-flower of the human body above in the eyes, that is the great key of the human body. Children, take heed! If for a day you do not practise meditation, this light streams out, who knows whither? If you only meditate for a quarter of an hour, by it you can do away with the ten thousand aeons and a thousand births. All methods end in quietness. This marvellous magic cannot be fathomed.

But when the practice is started, one must press on from the obvious to the profound, from the coarse to the fine. Everything depends on there being no interruption. The beginning and the end of the practice must be one. In between there are cooler and warmer moments, that goes without saying. But the goal must be to reach the vastness of heaven and the depths of the sea, so that all methods seem quite easy and taken for granted. Only then have we mastered it.

[1] *Huang-ti nei-ching su-wen*, a Taoist work of a later time which purports to come from the mythical ruler Huang Ti.

All holy men have bequeathed this to one another: nothing is possible without contemplation (*fan-chao*, reflection). When Confucius says: 'Perceiving brings one to the goal'; or when the Buddha calls it: 'The vision of the heart'; or Lao-tse says: 'Inner vision', it is all the same.

Anyone can talk about reflection, but he cannot master it if he does not know what the word means. What has to be reversed by reflection is the self-conscious heart, which has to direct itself towards that point where the formative spirit is not yet manifest. Within our six-foot body we must strive for the form which existed before the laying down of heaven and earth. If to-day people sit and meditate only one or two hours, looking only at their own egos, and call this reflection, how can anything come of it?

The two founders of Buddhism and Taoism have taught that one should look at the tip of one's nose. But they did not mean that one should fasten one's thoughts to the tip of the nose. Neither did they mean that, while the eyes were looking at the tip of the nose, the thoughts should be concentrated on the yellow middle. Wherever the eye looks, the heart is directed also. How can it be directed at the same time upward (yellow middle), and downward (tip of the nose), or alternatively, so that it is now up, now down? All that means confusing the finger with which one points to the moon with the moon itself.

What then is really meant by this? The expression 'tip of the nose' is very cleverly chosen. The nose must serve the eyes as a guide-line. If one is not guided by the nose, either one opens wide the eyes and looks into the distance, so that the nose is not seen, or the lids shut too much, so that the eyes close, and again the nose is not seen. But when the eyes are opened too wide, one makes the mistake of directing them outward, whereby one is easily distracted. If they are closed too much, one makes the mistake of letting them turn inward, whereby one easily sinks into a dreamy reverie. Only when the eyelids are lowered properly halfway is the tip of the nose seen in just the right way. Therefore it is taken as a guide-line. The main thing is to lower the eyelids in the right way, and then to allow the light to stream in of itself; without effort, wanting the light to stream in concentratedly. Looking at the tip of the nose serves only as the beginning of the inner concentration, so that the eyes are brought into the right direction for looking, and then are held to the guide-line: after that, one can let it be. That is the way a mason hangs up a plumb-line. As soon as he has hung it up, he guides his work by it without continually bothering himself to look at the plumb-line.

Fixating contemplation[1] is a Buddhist method which has not by any means been handed down as a secret.

One looks with both eyes at the tip of the nose, sits upright and in a comfortable position, and holds the heart to the centre in the midst of conditions. In Taoism it is called the yellow middle, in Buddhism the centre of the midst of conditions. The two are the same. It does not necessarily mean the middle of the head. It is only a matter of fixing one's thinking on the point which lies exactly between the two eyes. Then all is well. The light is something extremely mobile. When one fixes the thought on the mid-point between the two eyes, the light streams in of its own accord. It is not necessary to direct the attention especially to the central castle. In these few words the most important thing is contained.

'The centre in the midst of conditions' is a very subtle expression. The centre is omnipresent; everything is contained in it;

[1] The method of fixating contemplation (*chih-kuan*) is the meditation method of the Buddhist *T'ien-t'ai* school. It alternates between quieting emotions by breathing practices and by contemplation. In what follows, some of its methods are taken over. The 'conditions' are the circumstances, the 'environment', which, in conjunction with the 'causes' (yin), set going the circulation of delusion. The 'fixed pole in the flight of phenomena' is quite literally in the 'centre of conditions'.

it is connected with the release of the whole process of creation. The condition is the portal. The condition, that is, the fulfilment of this condition, makes the beginning, but it does not bring about the rest with inevitable necessity. The meaning of these two words is very fluid and subtle.

Fixating contemplation is indispensable; it ensures the making fast of the enlightenment. Only one must not stay sitting rigidly if worldly thoughts come up, but one must examine where the thought is, where it began, and where it fades out. Nothing is gained by pushing reflection further. One must be content to see where the thought arose, and not seek beyond the point of origin; for to find the heart (consciousness, to get behind consciousness with consciousness), that cannot be done. Together we want to bring the states of the heart to rest, that is true contemplation. What contradicts it is false contemplation. That leads to no goal. When the flight of the thoughts keeps extending further, one should stop and begin contemplating. Let one contemplate and then start fixating again. That is the double method of making fast the enlightenment. It means the circulation of the light. The circulation is fixation. The light is contemplation. Fixation without contemplation is circulation without light. Contemplation without fixation is light without circulation! Take note of that!

The general meaning of this section is that protection of the centre is important for the circulation of the light. The last section dealt with the theme that the human body is a very valuable possession when the primal spirit is master. But when it is used by the conscious spirit, the latter brings it about that, day and night, the primal spirit is scattered and wasted. When it is completely worn out, the body dies. Now the method is described whereby the conscious spirit can be subjected and the primal spirit protected; that is impossible if one does not begin by making the light circulate. It is like this: if a splendid house is to be erected, a fine foundation must first be built. When the foundation is firm, then only can the work proceed and the base of the walls be deeply and solidly

嬰兒現形圖

此時丹熟更須慈母惜嬰兒

氣穴法名無盡藏
藏包於窈窈包空
我問空中誰氏子
他云是你主人翁

行住坐臥
抱雌守雌
綿綿若存
念茲在茲

夫蠔蠣之虫
孕蟢蛤之子
俾其情交葉
精泝其氣栩
其神隨物大
小俱得其真

潛龍今已化飛龍
變現神通不可窮
一朝跳出珠光外
一浸身直到紫微官

神水溶液
沆瀣根休
內外無塵
長養聖胎

他日雲飛方見真人朝上帝

Meditation, Stage 2: Origin of a new being in the place of power.

grounded, and the pillars and walls built up. If a foundation is not laid in this way, how can the house be completed? The method of cultivating life is exactly like that. The circulation of the light is to be compared with the foundation of the building. When the foundation stands firm, how quickly it can be built upon! To protect the yellow middle with the fire of the spirit, that is the work of building. Therefore the Master makes especially clear the method by which one enters into the cultivation of life, and bids people look with both eyes at the tip of the nose, to lower the lids, to look within, sit quietly with upright body, and fix the heart on the centre in the midst of conditions.

Keeping the thoughts on the space between the two eyes allows the light to penetrate. Thereupon, the spirit crystallizes and enters the centre in the midst of conditions. The centre in the midst of conditions is the lower Elixir-field, the place of energy (solar plexus).

The Master hinted at this secretly when he said that at the beginning of practice one must sit in a quiet room, the body like dry wood, the heart like cooled ashes. Let the lids of both eyes be lowered; then look within and purify the heart, wash the thoughts, stop pleasures, and conserve the seed. Sit down daily to meditate with legs crossed. Let the light in the eyes be stopped; let the hearing power of the ear be crystallized and the tasting power of the tongue diminished; that is, the tongue should be laid to the roof of the mouth; let the breathing through the nose be made rhythmical and the thoughts fixed on the dark door. If the breathing is not first made rhythmical it is to be feared that there will be difficulty in breathing, because of stoppage. When one closes the eyes, then one should take as a measure a point on the bridge of the nose which lies not quite half an inch below the intersection point of the line of vision, where there is a little bump on the nose. Then one begins to collect one's thoughts; the ears make the breathing rhythmical; body and heart are comfortable and harmonious. The light of the eyes must shine quietly, and, for a long time, neither sleepiness nor distraction must set in. The eyes do not look forward, they lower their lids and light up what is within. It shines on this place. The mouth does not speak nor laugh. One closes the lips and breathes inwardly. Breathing is at this place. The nose smells no odours. Smelling is at this place. The ear does not hear things outside. Hearing is at this place. The whole heart watches over what is within. Its watching is at this place. The thoughts do not stray outward; true thoughts have duration in themselves. If the thoughts endure, the seed is enduring; if the seed endures, the energy endures; if the energy endures, then will the spirit endure. The spirit is thought; thought is the heart; the heart is the fire; the fire is the Elixir. When one looks at what is within in this way, the wonders of the opening and shutting of the gates of heaven will be inexhaustible. But the deeper secrets cannot be effected without making the breathing rhythmical.

If the pupil begins and cannot hold his thoughts to the place between the two eyes; if he closes the eyes, but the energy of the heart does not enable him to view the space of energy, the cause is most probably that the breathing is too loud and hasty, and other evils arise from this, because body and heart are kept busy trying to suppress forcibly the uprush of energy and quick breath.

If the thoughts are held only to the two eyes, but the spirit is not crystallized in the solar plexus (the centre in the midst of conditions), it is as if one had mounted to the hall but had not yet entered the inner chamber. Then the spirit-fire will not develop, the energy remains cold, and the true fruit will hardly manifest itself.

Therefore the Master harbours the fear lest, in their efforts, men only fix their thoughts on the place on the nose, but fail to think of fixing their ideas on the space of energy; that is why he used the comparison of the mason with the plumb-line. The mason uses the plumb-line only in order to see if his wall is perpendicular or slanting, and for this the string serves as a guide-line. When he has determined the direction, he can begin the work. But then he works on the wall, not on the plumb-line. That is clear. From this it is seen that fixing the thoughts between the eyes means only what the plumb-line does to the mason. The Master refers again and again to this because he fears his meaning might not be understood. And even if the pupils have grasped the way of doing the thing, he fears they might interrupt their work, and so he says several times: 'Only after a hundred days of consistent work, only then is the light genuine; only then can one begin work with the spirit-fire.' If one proceeds in a collected fashion, after a hundred days there develops spontaneously in the light a point of the genuine creative light (yang). The pupils must examine that with sincere hearts.

4. CIRCULATION OF THE LIGHT AND MAKING THE BREATHING RHYTHMICAL

Master Lü-tsu said, The decision must be carried out with a collected heart, and not seeking success; success will then come of itself. In the first period of release there are chiefly two mistakes: indolence and distraction. But that can be remedied; the heart must not enter into the breathing too completely. Breathing comes from the heart.[1] What comes out of the heart is breath. As soon as the heart stirs, there develops breath-energy. Breath-energy is originally transformed activity of the heart. When our ideas go very fast they imperceptibly pass into fantasies which are always accompanied by the drawing of a breath, because this inner and outer breathing hangs together like tone and echo. Daily we draw innumerable breaths and have an equal number of fantasies. And thus the clarity of the spirit ebbs away as wood dries out and ashes die.

So, then, should a man have no imaginings in his mind? One cannot be without imaginings. Should one not breathe? One cannot do without breathing. The best way is to make a medicine of the illness. Since heart and breath are mutually dependent, the circulation of the light must be united with the rhythm of breathing. For this, light of the ear is above all necessary. There is a light of the eye and a light of the ear. The light of the eye is the united light of the sun and moon outside. The light of the ear is the united seed of sun and moon within. The seed is thus the light in crystallized form. Both have the same origin and are different only in name. Therefore, understanding (ear) and clarity (eye) are one and the same effective light.

[1] The Chinese character for 'breath' (*hsi*) is made up of the character *tzu*, 'of', 'self', and the character *hsin*, 'heart' or 'consciousness'. Thus it can be interpreted as 'coming from the heart', 'having its origin in the heart', but at the same time it describes the condition in which 'the heart is at one with itself', i.e. quietness.

In sitting down, after lowering the lids, one uses the eyes to establish a plumb-line and then shifts the light downward. But if the transposition downward is not successful, then the heart is directed towards listening to the breathing. One should not be able to hear with the ear the outgoing and intaking of the breath. What one hears is that it has no tone. As soon as it has tone, the breathing is rough and superficial, and does not penetrate into the open. Then the heart must be made quite light and insignificant. The more it is released, the less it becomes; the less it is, the quieter. All at once it becomes so quiet that it stops. Then the true breathing is manifested and the form of the heart comes to consciousness. If the heart is light, the breathing is light, for every movement of the heart affects breath-energy. If breathing is light, the heart is light, for every movement of breath-energy affects the heart. In order to steady the heart, one begins by taking care of the breath-energy. The heart cannot be influenced directly. Therefore the breath-energy is used as a handle, and this is what is called maintenance of the concentrated breath-energy.

Children, do you not understand the nature of movement? Movement can be produced by outside means. It is only another name for mastery. One can make the heart move merely by running. Should one not also be able to bring it to rest by concentrated quietness? The great holy ones who knew how the heart and breath-energy mutually influence one another have thought out an easier procedure in order to help posterity.

In the *Book of the Elixir*[1] it is said: 'The hen can hatch her eggs because her heart is always listening.' That is an important magic spell. The hen can hatch the eggs because of the energy

[1] A secret book of the sects of the golden life-pill. (The legendary tradition of this book, *Tan-shu*, goes back very far; see Richard Wilhelm, *Das Buch der Sitte*, Jena, 1930, p. 302 [*Das Scharlachbuch*]. The present Taoist Canon no longer has a book by this title. H. W.)

of heat. But the energy of the heat can only warm the shells; it cannot penetrate into the interior. Therefore she conducts this energy inward with her heart. This she does with her hearing. In this way she concentrates her whole heart. When the heart penetrates, the energy penetrates, and the chick receives the energy of the heat and begins to live. Therefore a hen, even when at times she leaves her eggs, always has the attitude of listening with bent ear. Thus the concentration of the spirit is not interrupted. Because the concentration of the spirit suffers no interruption, neither does the energy of heat suffer interruption day or night, and the spirit awakens to life. The awakening of the spirit is accomplished because the heart has first died. When a man can let his heart die, then the primal spirit wakes to life. To kill the heart does not mean to let it dry and wither away, but it means that it has become un-divided and gathered into one.

The Buddha said: 'When you fix your heart on one point, then nothing is impossible for you.' The heart easily runs away, so it is necessary to concentrate it by means of breath-energy. Breath-energy easily becomes rough, therefore it has to be refined by the heart. When that is done, can it then happen that it is not fixed?

The two mistakes of indolence and distraction must be combated by quiet work that is carried on daily without interruption; then success will certainly be achieved. If one is not seated in meditation, one will often be distracted without noticing it. To become conscious of the distraction is the mechanism by which to do away with distraction. Indolence of which a man is conscious, and indolence of which he is unconscious, are a thousand miles apart. Unconscious indolence is real indolence; conscious indolence is not complete indolence, because there is still some clarity in it. Distraction comes from letting the mind wander about; indolence comes from the mind's not yet being pure. Distraction is much easier to correct than indolence. It is as in sickness: if one feels pains and irritations, one can help them with remedies, but indolence is like a disease that is attended by lack of realization. Distraction can be counteracted, confusion can be straightened out, but indolence and lethargy are heavy and dark. Distraction and confusion at least have a place, but in indolence and lethargy the anima alone is active. In distraction the animus is still present, but in indolence pure darkness rules. If one becomes sleepy during meditation, that is an effect of indolence. Only breathing serves to overcome indolence. Although the breath that flows in and out through the nose is not the true breath, the flowing in and out of the true breath takes place in connection with it.

While sitting, one must therefore always keep the heart quiet and the energy concentrated. How can the heart be made quiet? By the breath. Only the heart must be conscious of the flowing in and out of the breath; it must not be heard with the ears. If it is not heard, then the breathing is light; if light, it is pure. If it can be heard, then the breath-energy is rough; if rough, then it is troubled; if it is troubled, then indolence and lethargy develop and one wants to sleep. That is self-evident.

How to use the heart correctly during breathing must be understood. It is a use without use. One should only let the light fall quite gently on the hearing. This sentence contains a secret meaning. What does it mean to let the light fall? It is the spontaneous radiation of the light of the eyes. The eye looks inward only and not outward. To sense brightness without looking outward means to look inward; it has nothing to do with an actual looking within. What does hearing mean? It is the spontaneous hearing of the light of the ear. The ear listens inwardly only and does not listen to what is outside. To sense brightness without listening to what is outside is to listen inwardly; it has nothing to do with actually listening to what is within. In this sort of hearing, one hears only that there is no sound; in this kind of seeing, one sees only that no shape is there. If the eye is not looking outward and the ear is not hearkening outward, they close themselves and are inclined to sink inward. Only when one looks and hearkens inward does the organ not go outward nor sink inward. In this way indolence and lethargy are done away with. That is the union of the seed and the light of the sun and moon.

If, as a result of indolence, one becomes sleepy, one should stand up and walk about. When the mind has become clear one should sit down again. If there is time in the morning, one may sit during the burning of an incense stick, that is the best. In the afternoon, human affairs interfere and one can therefore easily fall into indolence. It is not necessary, however, to have an incense stick. But one must lay aside all entanglements and sit quite still for a time. In the course of time there will be success without one's becoming indolent and falling asleep.

The chief thought of this section is that the most important thing for achieving the circulation of the light is rhythmical breathing. The further the work advances, the deeper becomes the teaching. During the circulation of the light, the pupil must co-ordinate heart and breathing in order to avoid the annoyance of indolence and distraction. The Master fears that when beginners have once sat and lowered their lids, confused fantasies may arise, because of which, the heart will begin to beat so that it is difficult to guide. Therefore he teaches the practice of counting the breath and fixing the thoughts of the heart in order to prevent the energy of the spirit from flowing outward.

Because breath comes out of the heart, unrhythmical breathing comes from the heart's unrest. Therefore one must breathe in and out quite softly so that it remains inaudible to the ear, and only the heart quietly counts the breaths. When the heart forgets the number of breaths, that is a sign that the heart has gone off into the outer world. Then one must hold the heart steadfast. If the ear does not listen attentively, or the eyes do not look at the bridge of the nose, it often happens that the heart runs off outside, or that sleep comes.

That is a sign that the condition is going over into confusion and lethargy, and the seed-spirit must be brought into order again. If, in lowering the lids and taking direction from the nose, the mouth is not tightly closed and the teeth are not clenched firmly together, it can also easily happen that the heart hastens outward; then one must close the mouth quickly and clench the teeth. The five senses order themselves according to the heart, and the spirit must have recourse to breath-energy so that heart and breath are harmonized. In this way there is need at most of daily work of a few quarter-hours for heart and breathing to come of themselves into the right sort of collaboration and harmony. Then one need no longer count and breathing becomes rhythmical of its own accord. When the breathing is rhythmical the mistakes of indolence and distraction disappear in time of their own accord.

5. MISTAKES DURING THE CIRCULATION OF THE LIGHT

Master Lü-tsu said, Your work will gradually become concentrated and mature, but before you reach the condition in which you sit like a withered tree before a cliff, there are still many possibilities of error which I would like to bring to your special attention. These conditions are recognized only when they have been personally experienced. I shall enumerate them here. My school differs from the Buddhist yoga school (*Chan-tsung*)[1] in that it has confirmatory signs for each step of the way. First I would like to speak of the mistakes and then of the confirmatory signs.

When one begins to carry out one's decision, care must be taken so that everything can proceed in a comfortable, relaxed manner. Too much must not be demanded of the heart. One must be careful that, quite automatically, heart and energy are co-ordinated. Only then can a state of quietness be attained. During this quiet state the right conditions and the right space must be provided. One must not sit down [to meditate] in the

---

[1] In Japanese, *Zen*.

midst of frivolous affairs. That is to say, the mind must be free of vain preoccupations. All entanglements must be put aside; one must be detached and independent. Nor must the thoughts be concentrated upon the right procedure. This danger arises if too much trouble is taken. I do not mean that no trouble is to be taken, but the correct way lies in keeping equal distance between being and not being. If one can attain purposelessness through purpose, then the thing has been grasped. Now one can let oneself go, detached and without confusion, in an independent way.

Furthermore, one must not fall victim to the ensnaring world. The ensnaring world is where the five kinds of dark demons disport themselves. This is the case, for example, when, after fixation, one has chiefly thoughts of dry wood and dead ashes, and few thoughts of the bright spring on the great earth. In this way one sinks into the world of the dark. The energy is cold there, breathing is rough, and many images of coldness and decay present themselves. If one tarries there long one enters the world of plants and stones.

Nor must a man be led astray by the ten thousand ensnare-ments. This happens if, after the quiet state has begun, one after another all sorts of ties suddenly appear. One wants to break through them and cannot; one follows them, and feels as if relieved by this. This means the master has become the servant. If a man tarries in this stage long he enters the world of illusory desires.

At best, one finds oneself in heaven, at the worst, among the fox-spirits.[1] Such a fox-spirit, it is true, may be able to roam in the famous mountains enjoying the wind and the moon, the flowers and fruits, and taking his pleasure in coral trees and jewelled grass. But after having done this for three to five

---

[1] According to Chinese folk-lore, foxes can also cultivate the Elixir of Life; they thus attain the capacity of transforming themselves into human beings. They correspond to the nature demons of Western mythology.

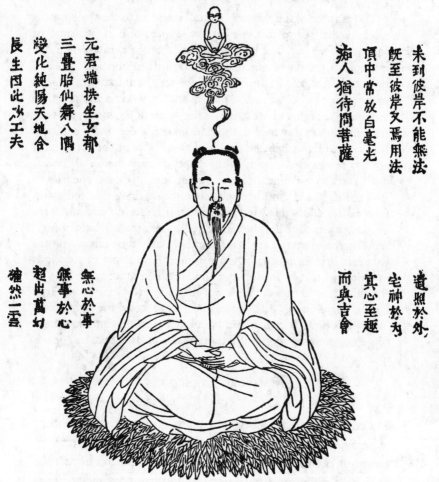

端拱冥心圖

長生因此功夫
三疊胎仙舞八佾
元君端拱坐玄都
變化純陽天地合

既至彼岸又焉用法
未到彼岸不能無法
頂中常放白毫光
痴人猶待問菩薩

雄然一吾
無心於事
無事於心
超出萬幻

道照於外
宅神於身
冥心至趣
而與言會

Meditation, Stage 3: Separation of the spirit-body for independent existence.

hundred years, or at the most for a couple of thousand years, his reward is over and he is born again into the world of turmoil.

All of these are wrong paths. When a man knows the wrong paths, he can then inquire into the confirmatory signs.

The purpose of this section[1] is to call attention to the wrong paths while meditating so that one enters the space of energy instead of the cave of fantasy. The latter is the world of the demons. This, for example, is the case if one sits down to meditate and sees flames of light or bright colours appear, or if one sees Bodhisattvas and gods approach, or any other similar phantasms. Or, if one is not successful in uniting energy and breathing, if the water of the kidneys cannot rise, but presses downward, the primal energy becoming cold and breathing rough: then the gentle light-energies of the great earth are too few, and one lands in the empty fantasy-world. Or, when one has sat a long time, and ideas rise up in crowds and one tries to stop them, but cannot; one submits to being driven by them and feels easier: when this happens, one must under no circumstances go on with meditation, but must get up and walk around a little until heart and energy are again in unison; only then can one return to meditation. In meditating, a man must have a sort of conscious intuition, so that he feels energy and breathing unite in the field of the Elixir; he must feel that a warm release belonging to the true light is beginning to stir dimly. Then he has found the right space. When this right space has been found, one is freed from the danger of getting into the world of illusory desire or dark demons.

6. CONFIRMATORY EXPERIENCES DURING THE CIRCULATION OF THE LIGHT

Master Lü-tsu said, There are many kinds of confirmatory experiences. One must not content oneself with small demands but must rise to the thought that all living creatures have to be redeemed. One must not be trivial and irresponsible in heart, but must strive to make deeds prove one's words.

[1] This section shows plainly a Buddhist influence. The temptation mentioned here consists in one's being impelled by such fantasies to take them as real, and to succumb to them. (Compare the scene where Mephistopheles puts Faust to sleep by means of his demons.)

If, when there is quiet, the spirit has continuously and uninterruptedly a sense of great joy as if intoxicated or freshly bathed, it is a sign that the light-principle is harmonious in the whole body; then the Golden Flower begins to bud. When, furthermore, all openings are quiet, and the silver moon stands in the middle of heaven, and one has the feeling that this great earth is a world of light and brightness, that is a sign that the body of the heart opens itself to clarity. It is a sign that the Golden Flower is opening.

Furthermore, the whole body feels strong and firm so that it fears neither storm nor frost. Things by which other men are displeased, when I meet them, cannot becloud the brightness of the seed of the spirit. Yellow gold fills the house; the steps are of white jade. Rotten and stinking things on earth that come in contact with one breath of the true energy will immediately live again. Red blood becomes milk. The fragile body of the flesh is sheer gold and diamonds. That is a sign that the Golden Flower is crystallized.

The *Book of Successful Contemplation* (*Ying-kuan-ching*) says: 'The sun sinks in the great water and magic pictures of trees in rows arise.' The setting of the sun means that in chaos (in the world before phenomena, that is before the intelligible world) the foundation is laid: that is the non-polarized condition [ultimateless] (*wu-chi*). Highest good is like water, pure and spotless. It is the ruler of the great polarity, the god who appears in the trigram of shock, *Chen*.[1] *Chen* is also symbolized

[1] Compare the *I Ching*, section *Shuo Kua* (Discussion of the Trigrams). *Chen* is the trigram for thunder, spring, east, wood. The Creative, heaven, is in the northwest in this arrangement. The Abysmal is in the north.

K'an, the Abysmal, water, the moon

Ch'ien, the Creative, heaven

Ken, Keeping Still, the mountain, stillness

Tui, the Joyous, lake, mist

Chen, the Arousing, wood, thunder

K'un, the Receptive, earth

Sun, the Gentle, wind, the penetrating

Li, the Clinging, fire, light, sun, warmth

by wood, and so the image of trees in rows appears. A seven-fold row of trees means the light of the seven body-openings (or heart-openings). The northwest is the direction of the Creative. When it moves on one place further, the Abysmal is there. The sun which sinks into the great water is the image for the Creative and the Abysmal. The Abysmal is the direction of midnight (mouse, *tzu*, north). At the winter solstice, thunder (*Chen*) is in the middle of the earth quite hidden and covered up. Only when the trigram *Chen* is reached does the light-pole appear over the earth again. That is the image represented by the rows of trees. The rest can be correspondingly inferred.

The second part means the building of the foundation on this. The great world is like ice, a glassy jewel-world. The brilliancy of the light gradually crystallizes. Hence a great terrace arises and upon it, in the course of time, the Buddha appears. When the golden being appears who should it be but the Buddha? For the Buddha is the golden holy man of the great enlightenment. This is a great confirmatory experience.

Now there are three confirmatory experiences which can be tested. The first is that, when one has entered the state of meditation, the gods are in the valley.[1] Men are heard talking as though at a distance of several hundred paces, each one quite clear. But the sounds are all like an echo in a valley. One can always hear them, but never oneself. This is called the presence of the gods in the valley.

At times the following can be experienced: as soon as one is quiet, the light of the eyes begins to blaze up, so that everything before one becomes quite bright as if one were in a cloud. If one opens one's eyes and seeks the body, it is not to be found any more. This is called: 'In the empty chamber it grows

[1] Compare Lao-tse, *Tao Te Ching*, section 6. (Arthur Waley has translated this work: *The Way and Its Power*, London and New York. There is a paperback edition in the Evergreen Series, New York. C. F. B.)

light.' Inside and outside, everything is equally light. That is a very favourable sign.

Or, when one sits in meditation, the fleshly body becomes quite shining like silk or jade. It seems difficult to remain sitting; one feels as if drawn upward. This is called: 'The spirit returns and touches heaven.' In time, one can experience it in such a way that one really floats upward.

And now, it is already possible to have all three of these experiences. But not everything can be expressed. Different things appear to each person according to his disposition. If one experiences these things, it is a sign of a good aptitude. With these things it is just as it is when one drinks water. One can tell for oneself whether the water is warm or cold. In the same way a man must convince himself about these experiences, then only are they real.

7. THE LIVING MANNER OF THE CIRCULATION OF THE LIGHT

Master Lü-tsu said, When there is a gradual success in producing the circulation of the light, a man must not give up his ordinary occupation in doing it. The ancients said, When occupations come to us, we must accept them; when things come to us, we must understand them from the ground up. If the occupations are properly handled by correct thoughts, the light is not scattered by outside things, but circulates according to its own law. Even the still invisible circulation of the light gets started this way; how much more, then, is it the case with the true circulation of the light which has already manifested itself clearly.

When in ordinary life one has the ability always to react to things by reflexes only, without any admixture of a thought of others or of oneself, that is a circulation of the light arising out of circumstances. This is the first secret.

If, early in the morning, one can rid oneself of all entanglements and meditate from one to two double hours, and then can orientate oneself towards all activities and outside things in a purely objective, reflex way, and if this can be continued without any interruption, then after two or three months all the perfected ones come from heaven and approve such behaviour.

The preceding section deals with the blissful fields that are entered when one goes forward in the work. The aim of this section is to show the pupils how they must shape their work more subtly day by day so that they may hope for an early attainment of the Elixir of Life. How does it happen that the Master just at this point speaks of the fact that a man ought not to give up his ordinary way of life? It might be thought from this that the Master wanted to prevent the pupil from attaining the Elixir of Life quickly. He who knows replies to this, Not at all! The Master is concerned lest the pupil may not have fulfilled his karma, therefore he speaks in this way. Now if the work has already led into the blissful fields, the heart is like an expanse of water. When things come, it mirrors things; when things go, spirit and energy spontaneously unite again and do not allow themselves to be carried away by externals. That is what the Master means when he says that every entanglement in thought of other people and oneself must be completely given up. When the pupil succeeds in concentrating with true thoughts always on the space of energy, he does not have to start the light rotating, and the light rotates by itself. But when the light rotates, the Elixir is made spontaneously, and the performance of worldly tasks at the same time is not a hindrance. It is different at the beginning of the practice of meditation when spirit and energy are still scattered and confused. If worldly affairs cannot then be kept at a distance and a quiet place be found where one can concentrate with all one's energy, and thus avoid all disturbances from ordinary occupations, then one is perhaps industrious in the morning and certainly indolent in the evening. How long would it take till a man attained to the real secrets in this way? Therefore it is said, When one begins to apply oneself to the work, one should put aside household affairs. And, if that is not wholly possible, someone ought to be engaged to look after them so that one can take pains with complete attention. But when the work is so far advanced that secret confirmations are experienced, it does not matter if, at the same time, one's ordinary affairs are put in order, so that one can fulfil one's karma. This means the living manner of the circulation of the light. Long ago, the True Man of the Purple Polar Light (Tzu-yang chen-jen)[1] said a word: 'If one cultivates one's action while mingling with the world and is still in harmony with the light, then the round is round and the angular has angles; then he lives among men, mysterious yet visible, different and yet the same, and none can compass it; then no one notices our secret actions.' The living manner of the circulation of the light has just this meaning: to live mingling with the world and yet in harmony with the light.

8. A MAGIC SPELL FOR THE FAR JOURNEY[2]

Master Lü-tsu said, Yü Ch'ing has left behind him a magic spell for the far journey:

Four words crystallize the spirit in the space of energy.
In the sixth month white snow is suddenly seen to fly.
At the third watch the sun's disk sends out blinding
rays.
In the water blows the wind of the Gentle.
Wandering in heaven, one eats the spirit-energy of
the Receptive.
And the still deeper secret of the secret:
The land that is nowhere, that is the true home . . .

These verses are full of mystery. The meaning is: The most important things in the great Tao are the words: action through non-action. Non-action prevents a man from becoming entangled in form and image (materiality). Action in non-

[1] There are several Taoist adepts bearing this name. The one referred to here is probably Chang Po-tuan, who lived in the eleventh century A.D. On him and on his writings compare Tenney L. Davis and Chao Yünts'ung in: *Proceedings of the American Academy of Arts and Sciences*, 73, 5 (1939), pp. 97-117, and 73, 13 (1940), pp. 371-399. (H. W.)

[2] The reference is to the first chapter of *Chuang-tzu*. (H. W.)

action prevents a man from sinking into numbing emptiness and dead nothingness. The effect depends entirely on the central One; the releasing of the effect is in the two eyes. The two eyes are like the pole of the Great Wain which turns the whole of creation; they cause the poles of light and darkness to circulate. The Elixir depends from beginning to end on one thing: the metal in the midst of the water, that is, the lead in the water-region. Heretofore we have spoken of the circulation of the light, indicating thereby the initial release which works from without upon what lies within. This is to aid one in obtaining the Master. It is for pupils in the beginning stages. They go through the two lower transitions in order to gain the upper one. After the sequence of events is clear and the nature of the release is known, heaven no longer withholds the Way, but reveals the ultimate truth. Disciples, keep it secret and redouble your effort!

The circulation of the light is the inclusive term. The further the work advances, the more does the Golden Flower bloom. But there is a still more marvellous kind of circulation. Till now we have worked from the outside on what is within; now we stay in the centre and rule what is external. Hitherto it was a service in aid of the Master; now it is a dissemination of the commands of the Master. The whole relationship is now reversed. If one wants to penetrate the more subtle regions by this method, one must first see to it that body and heart are completely controlled, that one is quite free and at peace, letting go of all entanglements, untroubled by the slightest excitement, and with the heavenly heart exactly in the middle. Then let one lower the lids of the two eyes as if one received a holy edict, a summons to become the minister. Who would dare disobey? Then with both eyes one illumines the house of the Abysmal (water, *K'an*). Wherever the Golden Flower goes, the true light of polarity comes forth to meet it. The Clinging (brightness, *Li*) is bright outside and dark within; this is the body of the Creative. The one dark [line] enters and becomes master. The result is that the heart (consciousness) develops in dependence on things, is directed outward, and is tossed about on the stream. When the rotating light shines towards what is within, it does not develop in dependence on things, the energy of the dark is fixed, and the Golden Flower shines concentratedly. This is then the collected light of polarity. Related things attract each other. Thus the polarized light-line of the Abysmal presses upward. It is not only the light in the abyss, but it is creative light which meets creative light. As soon as these two substances meet each other, they unite inseparably, and there develops an unceasing life; it comes and goes, rises and falls of itself, in the house of the primal energy. One is aware of effulgence and infinity. The whole body feels light and would like to fly. This is the state of which it is said: Clouds fill the thousand mountains. Gradually it goes to and fro quite softly; it rises and falls imperceptibly. The pulse stands still and breathing stops. This is the moment of true creative union, the state of which it is said: The moon gathers up the ten thousand waters. In the midst of this darkness, the heavenly heart suddenly begins a movement. This is the return of the one light, the time when the child comes to life.

However, the details of this must be carefully explained. When a person looks at something, listens to something, eyes and ears move and follow the things until they have passed. These movements are all underlings, and when the heavenly ruler follows them in their tasks it means: to live together with demons.

If now, during every movement and every moment of rest, a person lives together with people and not with demons, then the heavenly ruler is the true man. When he moves, and we move with him, then the movement is the root of heaven. When he is quiet, and we are quiet with him, then this quiet-ness is the cave of the moon. When he unceasingly alternates movement and rest, go on with him unceasingly in movement and quietness. When he rises and falls with inhaling and exhaling, rise and fall with him. That is what is called going to and fro between the root of heaven and the cave of the moon.

When the heavenly heart still preserves calm, movement before the right time is a fault of softness. When the heavenly heart has already moved, the movement that follows afterwards, in order to correspond with it, is a fault of rigidity. As soon as the heavenly heart is stirring, one must immediately mount upward whole-heartedly to the house of the Creative. Thus the spirit-light sees the summit; this is the leader. This movement is in accord with the time. The heavenly heart rises to the summit of the Creative, where it expands in complete freedom. Then suddenly it demands the deepest silence, and one must lead it speedily and whole-heartedly into the yellow castle; thus the eyes behold the central yellow dwelling place of the spirit.

When the desire for silence comes, not a single thought arises; he who is looking inward suddenly forgets that he is looking. At this time, body and heart must be left completely released. All entanglements have disappeared without trace. Then I no longer know at what place the house of my spirit and my crucible are. If a man wants to make certain of his body, he cannot get at it. This condition is the penetration of heaven into earth, the time when all wonders return to their roots. So it is when the crystallized spirit goes into the space of energy.

The One is the circulation of the light. When one begins, it is at first still scattered and one wants to collect it; the six senses are not active. This is the cultivation and nourishment of one's own origin, the filling up of the oil when one goes to receive life. When one is far enough to have gathered it, one feels light and free and need not take the least trouble. This is the

Meditation, Stage 4: The centre in the midst of the conditions.

quieting of the spirit in the space of the ancestors, the taking possession of former heaven.

When one is so far advanced that every shadow and every echo has disappeared, so that one is entirely quiet and firm, this is refuge within the cave of energy, where all that is miraculous returns to its roots. One does not alter the place, but the place divides itself. This is incorporeal space where a thousand and ten thousand places are one place. One does not alter the time, but the time divides itself. This is immeasurable time when all the aeons are like a moment.

As long as the heart has not attained absolute tranquillity, it cannot move itself. One moves the movement and forgets the movement; this is not movement in itself. Therefore it is said: If, when stimulated by external things, one moves, it is the impulse of the being. If, when not stimulated by external things, one moves, it is the movement of heaven. The being that is placed over against heaven can fall and come under the domination of the impulses. The impulses are based upon the fact that there are external things. They are thoughts that go on beyond one's own position. Then movement leads to movement. But when no idea arises, the right ideas come. That is the true idea. When things are quiet and one is quite firm, and the release of heaven suddenly moves, is this not a movement without purpose? Action through non-action has just this meaning.

As to the poem at the beginning, the two first lines refer entirely to the activity of the Golden Flower. The two next lines are concerned with the mutual interpenetration of sun and moon. The sixth month is the Clinging (*Li*, fire). The white snow that flies is the true polar darkness in the middle of the fire trigram, that is about to turn into the Receptive. The third watch is the Abysmal (*K'an*, water). The sun's disk is the one polar line in the trigram for water, which is about to turn into the Creative. This contains the way to take the trigram for the

Abysmal and the way to reverse the trigram for the Clinging (fire, *Li*).

The following two lines have to do with the activity of the pole of the Great Wain, the rise and fall of the whole release of polarity. Water is the trigram of the Abysmal; the eye is the wind of the Gentle (*Sun*). The light of the eyes illumines the house of the Abysmal, and controls there the seed of the great light. 'In heaven', this means the house of the Creative (*Ch'ien*). 'Wandering in heaven, one eats the spirit-energy of the Receptive.' This shows how the spirit penetrates the energy, how heaven penetrates the earth; this happens so that the fire can be nourished.

Finally, the two last lines point to the deepest secret, which cannot be dispensed with from the beginning to the end. This is the washing of the heart and the purification of the thoughts; this is the bath. The holy science takes as a beginning the knowledge of where to stop, and as an end, stopping at the highest good. Its beginning is beyond polarity and it empties again beyond polarity.

The Buddha speaks of the transient, the creator of consciousness, as being the fundamental truth of religion. And the whole work of completing life and human nature in our Taoism lies in the expression 'to bring about emptiness'. All three religions agree in the one proposition, the finding of the spiritual Elixir in order to pass from death to life. In what does this spiritual Elixir consist? It means forever dwelling in purposelessness. The deepest secret of the bath that is to be found in our teaching is thus confined to the work of making the heart empty. Therewith the matter is settled. What I have revealed here in a word is the fruit of a decade of effort.

If you are not yet clear as to how far all three sections can be present in one section, I will make it clear to you through the threefold Buddhist contemplation of emptiness, delusion, and the centre.

Emptiness comes as the first of the three contemplations. All things are looked upon as empty. Then follows delusion. Although it is known that they are empty, things are not destroyed, but one attends to one's affairs in the midst of the emptiness. But though one does not destroy things, neither does one pay attention to them; this is contemplation of the centre. While practising contemplation of the empty, one also knows that one cannot destroy the ten thousand things, and still one does not notice them. In this way the three contemplations fall together. But, after all, strength is in envisioning the empty. Therefore, when one practises contemplation of emptiness, emptiness is certainly empty, but delusion is empty too, and the centre is empty. It needs a great strength to practise contemplation of delusion; then delusion is really delusion, but emptiness is also delusion, and the centre is delusion too. Being on the way of the centre, one also creates images of the emptiness; they are not called empty, but are called central. One practises also contemplation of delusion, but one does not call it delusion, one calls it central. As to what has to do with the centre, more need not be said.

This section mentions first Yü Ch'ing's magical spell for the far journey. This magical spell states that the secret wonder of the Way is how something develops out of nothing. In that spirit and energy unite in crystallized form, there appears, in the course of time, in the midst of the emptiness of nothing, a point of the true fire. During this time the more quiet the spirit becomes, the brighter is the fire. The brightness of the fire is compared with the sun's heat in the sixth month. Because the blazing fire causes the water of the Abysmal to vaporize, the steam is heated, and when it has passed the boiling point it mounts upward like flying snow. It is meant by this that one may see snow fly in the sixth month. But because the water is vaporized by the fire, the true energy is awakened; yet when the dark is at rest, the light begins to move; it is like the state of midnight. Therefore adepts call this time the time of the living midnight. At this time one works at the energy with the purpose of making it flow backward and rise, and flow down to fall like the upward spinning of the sun-wheel. Therefore it is said: 'At the third watch the sun's disk sends out blinding rays.' The rotation method makes use of breathing to blow on the fire of the gates of life; in this way one succeeds in bringing the true energy to its original place. Therefore it is said that the wind blows in the water. Out of the single energy of former heaven, there develops the out- and in-going breath of later heaven and its inflaming energy.

The way leads from the sacrum upward in a backward-flowing way to the summit of the Creative, and on through the house of the Creative; then it sinks through the two stories in a direct downward-flowing way into the solar plexus, and warms it. Therefore it is said: 'Wandering in heaven, one eats the spirit-energy of the Receptive.' Because the true energy goes back into the empty place, in time, energy and form become rich and full, body and heart become glad and cheerful. If, by the practice of the turning of the wheel of the doctrine, this cannot be achieved, how otherwise should one be able to enter upon this far journey? What it amounts to is this: the crystallized spirit radiates back to the spirit-fire and, by means of the greatest quiet, fans the 'fire in the midst of the water', which is in the middle of the empty cave. Therefore it is said: 'And the still deeper secret of the secret: the land that is nowhere, that is the true home.'

The pupil has already penetrated in his work into mysterious territory; but if he does not know the method of melting, it is to be feared that the Elixir of Life will hardly be produced. Therefore the Master has revealed the secret strictly guarded by the former holy men. When the pupil keeps the crystallized spirit fixed within the cave of energy and, at the same time, lets greatest quietness hold sway, then out of the obscure darkness a something develops from the nothingness, that is, the Golden Flower of the great One appears. At this time the conscious light is differentiated from the light of human nature [*hsing*]. Therefore it is said: 'To move when stimulated by external things leads to its going directly outward and creating a man. That is the conscious light.' If, at the time the true energy has been sufficiently collected, the pupil does not let it flow directly outward, but makes it flow backward, that is the light of life; the method of the turning of the water-wheel must be applied. If one continues to turn, the true energy returns to the roots, drop by drop. Then the water-wheel stops, the body is clean, the energy is fresh. One single turning means one heavenly cycle, what Master Ch'iu has called a small heavenly cycle. If one does not wait to use the energy until it has been collected sufficiently, it is then too tender and weak, and the Elixir is not formed. If the energy is there and not used, then it becomes too old and rigid, and then, too, the Elixir of Life will hardly be produced. When it is neither too old nor too tender, then is the right time to use it purposefully. This is what the Buddha means when he says: 'The phenomenon flows into emptiness.' This is the sublimation of the seed into energy. If the pupil does not understand this principle, and lets the energy flow out directly, then the energy changes into seed; this is what is meant when it is said: 'Emptiness finally flows into phenomena.' But every man who unites bodily with a woman feels pleasure first and then bitterness; when the seed has flowed out, the body is tired and the spirit weary. It is quite different when the adept lets spirit and energy unite. That brings first purity and then freshness; when the seed is transformed, the body is healthy and free. There is a tradition that the old Master P'eng grew to be eight hundred years old because he made use of serving maids to nourish his life, but that is a misunderstanding. In reality, he used the method of sublimation of spirit and energy. In the Elixir of Life symbols are used for the most part, and in them the fire of the Clinging (*Li*) is frequently compared to a bride, and the water of the Abyss to the boy (*puer aeternus*). From this arose the misunderstanding about Master P'eng having restored his virility through women. These are errors that have forced their way in later.

But adepts can use the means of overthrowing the Abysmal (*K'an*) and the Clinging (*Li*) only when they have sincere intention in the work, otherwise a pure mixture cannot be produced. The true purpose is subject to the earth; the colour of the earth is yellow, therefore in books on the Elixir of Life it is symbolized by the yellow germ. When the Abysmal and the Clinging (*Li*) unite, the Golden Flower appears; the golden colour is white, and therefore white snow is used as a symbol. But worldly people who do not understand the secret words of the *Book of the Elixir of Life* have misunderstood the yellow and white there in that they have taken it as a means of making gold out of stones. Is not that foolish?

An ancient adept said: 'Formerly, every school knew this jewel, only fools did not know it wholly.' If we reflect on this we see that the ancients really attained long life by the help of the seed-energy present in their own bodies, and did not lengthen their years by swallowing this or that sort of elixir. But the worldly people lost the roots and clung to the tree-tops. The *Book of the Elixir* also says: 'When the right man (white magician) makes use of wrong means, the wrong means work in the right way.' By this is meant the transformation of seed into energy. 'But if the wrong man uses the right means, the right means work in the wrong way.' By this is meant the bodily union of man and woman from which spring sons and daughters. The fool wastes the most precious jewel of his body in uncontrolled lust, and does not know how to conserve his seed-energy. When it is finished, the body perishes. The holy and wise men have no other way of cultivating their lives except by destroying lusts and safeguarding the seed. The accumulated seed is transformed into energy, and the energy, when there is enough of it, makes the creatively strong body. The difference shown by ordinary people depends only upon how they apply the downward-flowing way or the backward-flowing way.

The whole meaning of this section is directed towards making clear to the pupil the method of filling up the oil when meeting life. Here the eyes are the chief thing. The two eyes are the handle of the polar star. Even as heaven turns about the polar star as a centre point, so among men the right intention must be the master. Therefore the completion of the Elixir of Life depends entirely on the harmonizing of the right purpose. Then, if it is said that the foundation can be laid in a hundred days, first of all the degree of industry in work and the degree of strength in the physical constitution must be taken into account. Whoever is eager in the work, and has a strong constitution, succeeds more quickly in turning the water-wheel of the rear river. When a person has found the method of making thoughts and energy harmonize with one another, he can complete the Elixir within the hundred days. But whoever is weak and inert will not produce it even after the hundred days. When the Elixir is completed, spirit and energy are pure and clear; the heart is empty, human nature (*hsing*) manifest, and the light of consciousness transforms itself into the light of human nature. If one continues to hold firmly the light of human nature, the Abysmal and the Clinging (fire, *Li*) have intercourse spontaneously. When the Abysmal and the Clinging commingle, the holy fruit is borne.

63

The ripening of the holy fruit is the effect of a great heavenly cycle. Further elucidation stops with the method of the heavenly cycle.

This book is concerned with the means of cultivating life and shows at first how to start by looking at the bridge of one's nose; here the method of reversing is shown; the methods of making firm and letting go are in another book, the *Hsü Ming Fang*[1] (*Methods of Prolonging Life*).

Summary[2] of the Chinese Concepts on Which Is Based the Idea of the Golden Flower, or Immortal Spirit-Body

The Tao, the undivided, great One, gives rise to two opposite reality principles, the dark and the light, yin and yang. These are at first thought of only as forces of nature apart from man. Later, the sexual polarities and others as well are derived from them. From yin comes *K'un*, the receptive feminine principle; from yang comes *Ch'ien*, the creative masculine principle; from yin comes *ming*, life; from yang, *hsing* or human nature.

Each individual contains a central monad, which, at the moment of conception, splits into life and human nature, *ming* and *hsing*. These two are supra-individual principles, and so can be related to eros and logos.

In the personal bodily existence of the individual they are represented by two other polarities, a *p'o* soul (or anima) and a *hun* soul (animus). All during the life of the individual these two are in conflict, each striving for mastery. At death they separate and go different ways. The anima sinks to earth as *kuei*, a ghost-being. The animus rises and becomes *shen*, a spirit or god. *Shen* may in time return to the Tao.

If the life-energy flows downward, that is, without let or hindrance into the outer world, the anima is victorious over

---

[1] Another name for the *Hui Ming Ching*. (H. W.)

[2] This summary and the following diagram have been arranged for the English edition by the translator. (C. F. B.)

the animus; no spirit-body or Golden Flower is developed, and at death the ego is lost. If the life-energy is led through the 'backward-flowing' process, that is, conserved, and made to 'rise' instead of allowed to dissipate, the animus has been victorious, and the ego persists after death. It then becomes *shen*, a spirit or god. A man who holds to the way of conservation all through life may reach the stage of the Golden Flower, which then frees the ego from the conflict of the opposites, and it again becomes part of the Tao, the undivided, great One.

Diagram of the Chinese concepts concerned with the development of the Golden Flower, or immortal spirit-body

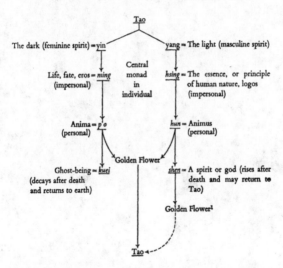

[1] As there is ample evidence in the text to show that Buddhist influences represented the Golden Flower as coming ultimately only from the spiritual side, that fact has been indicated by the dotted line leading down from *shen*. However, in undiluted Chinese teaching, the creation of the Golden Flower depends on the equal interplay of both the yang and the yin forces. (C. F. B.)

THE HUI MING CHING
The Book of Consciousness and Life

1. Cessation of Outflowing

If thou wouldst complete the diamond body with
  no outflowing,
Diligently heat the roots of consciousness and life.
Kindle light in the blessed country ever close at hand,
And there hidden, let thy true self always dwell.

The illustration found here in the Chinese text shows the body of a man. In the middle of the lower half of the body is drawn a germ cell by which the gateway of life is separated from the gateway of consciousness. In between, leading to the outside world, is the canal through which the vital fluids flow out.[1]

The subtlest secret of the Tao is human nature and life (hsing-ming). There is no better way of cultivating human nature and life than to bring both back to unity. The holy men of ancient times, and the great sages, set forth their thoughts about the unification of human nature and life by means of images from the external world; they were reluctant to speak of it openly without allegories. Therefore the secret of how to cultivate both simultaneously was lost on earth. What I show through a series of images is not a frivolous giving away of secrets. On the contrary, because I combined the notes of the Leng-yen-ching on the cessation of outflowing and the secret thoughts of Hua-yen-ching with occasional references to the other sutras, in order to summarize them in this true picture, it can be understood that consciousness and life are not anything external to the germinal vesicle. I have drawn this picture so that companions pursuing the divine workings of the dual

[1] This explanatory note and those that follow were contributed by Richard Wilhelm. (C. F. B.)

cultivation may know that in this way the true seed matures, that in this way the cessation of outflowing is brought about, that in this way the *sheli*[1] is melted out, that in this way the great Tao is completed.

But the germinal vesicle is an invisible cavern; it has neither form nor image. When the vital breath stirs, the seed of this vesicle comes into being; when it ceases it disappears again. It is the place which harbours truth, the altar upon which consciousness and life are made. It is called the dragon castle at the bottom of the sea, the boundary region of the snow mountains, the primordial pass, the kingdom of greatest joy, the boundless country. All these different names mean this germinal vesicle. If a dying man does not know this germinal vesicle, he will not find the unity of consciousness and life in a thousand births, nor in ten thousand aeons.

This germinal point is something great. Before this our body is born of our parents, at the time of conception, this seed is first created and human nature and life dwell therein. The two are intermingled and form a unity, inseparably mixed like the sparks in the refining furnace, a combination of primordial harmony and divine law. Therefore it is said: 'In the state before the appearance there is an inexhaustible breath.' Furthermore it is said: 'Before the parents have begotten the child, the breath of life is complete and the embryo perfect.' But when the embryo moves and the embryo vesicle is torn, it is as if a man lost his footing on a high mountain: with a cry the man plunges down to earth, and from then on human nature and life are divided. From this moment human nature can no longer see life nor life human nature. And now fate takes its course: youth passes over into maturity, maturity into old age, and old age into woe.

Therefore the Julai,[2] in his great compassion, let the secret

---

[1] *Sarira*, the firm, that is, the immortal body.
[2] The Buddha Tathagata.

making and melting be made known. He teaches one to re-enter the womb and create anew the human nature and life of the ego; he shows how spirit and soul (vital breath) enter the germinal vesicle, how they must combine to become a unity in order to complete the true fruit, just as the sperm[1] and soul of father and mother entered this germinal vesicle and united as one being in order to complete the embryo. The principle is the same.

Within the germinal vesicle is the fire of the ruler; at the entrance of the germinal vesicle is the fire of the minister; in the whole body, the fire of the people. When the fire of the ruler expresses itself, it is received by the fire of the minister. When the fire of the minister moves, the fire of the people follows him. When the three fires express themselves in this order a man develops. But when the three fires return in reverse order the Tao develops.

This is the reason that all the sages began their work at the germinal vesicle in which outflowing had ceased. If one does not establish this path, but sets up other things, it is of no avail. Therefore all the schools and sects which do not know that the ruling principle of consciousness and life is in this germinal vesicle, and which therefore seek it in the outer world, can accomplish nothing despite all their efforts to find it outside.

2. The Six Periods of Circulation in Conformity with the Law[2]

If one discerns the beginning of the Buddha's path,
There will be the blessed city of the West.

---

[1] *Ching*, the sperm, is the masculine element; *ch'i*, soul, breath-energy, is the feminine, receptive element.

[2] This concept has been borrowed from Buddhist terminology, in the context of which it is usually translated as the 'Wheel of the Law'. (H. W.)

After the circulation in conformity with the law,
   there is a turn upward towards heaven when the
   breath is drawn in.
When the breath flows out energy is directed towards
   the earth.
One time-period consists of six intervals (*hou*).
In two intervals one gathers Moni (Sakyamuni).
The great Tao comes forth from the centre.
Do not seek the primordial seed outside!

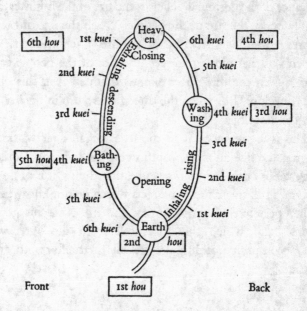

The most marvellous effect of the Tao is the circulation in conformity with the law. What makes the movement inexhaustible is the path. What best regulates the speed are the rhythms (*kuei*). What best determines the number of the exercises is the method of the intervals (*hou*).

This presentation contains the whole law, and the true features of the Buddha from the West are contained in it. The secrets contained in it show how one gets control of the process by exhaling and inhaling, how the alternation between decrease and increase expresses itself in closing and opening, how one needs true thoughts in order not to deviate from the way, how the firm delimitation of the regions makes it possible to begin and to stop at the right time.

I sacrifice myself and serve man, because I have presented fully this picture which reveals the heavenly seed completely, so that every layman and man of the world can reach it and so bring it to completion. He who lacks the right virtue may well find something in it, but heaven will not grant him his Tao. Why not? The right virtue belongs to the Tao as does one wing of a bird to the other: if one is lacking, the other is of no use. Therefore there is needed loyalty and reverence, humaneness and justice and strict adherence to the five commandments[1]; then only does one have the prospect of attaining something.

But all the subtleties and secrets are offered in this *Book of Consciousness and Life* to be pondered and weighed, so that one can attain everything in its truth.

The drawing is intended to show the circulation of the streams of energy during the movement of breathing. Inhalation is accompanied by the sinking of the abdomen and exhalation by the lifting of it, but in these exercises the point is that we have a backward-flowing movement as follows: when inhaling, one opens the lower energy-gate and allows the energy to rise upward along the rear line of energy (in the spinal cord), and this upward flow corresponds to the time-intervals indicated in the drawing. In exhaling, the upper gate is closed and the stream of energy is allowed to flow downward along the front line, likewise in the order of the time-intervals indicated. Furthermore, it is to be noted that the stations for 'washing' and 'bathing' do not lie exactly in the middle of the lines, but that 'washing' is somewhat above and 'bathing' somewhat below the middle, as the drawing shows.

[1] The Buddhist five commandments are: (1) not to kill; (2) not to steal; (3) not to commit adultery; (4) not to lie; (5) not to drink and not to eat meat.

3. The Two Energy-Paths of Function and Control

There appears the way of the in-breathing and out-
    breathing of the primordial pass.
Do not forget the white path below the circulation
    in conformity with the law!
Always let the cave of eternal life be nourished
    through the fire!
Ah! Test the immortal place of the gleaming pearl!

In the text there is another picture here which is very similar to the first. It shows again the paths of energy: the one in front leads down and is called the function-path (*jen*), and the one at the back leading upwards is the control-path (*tu*).

This picture is really the same as the one that precedes it. The reason that I show it again is so that the person striving for cultivation of the Tao may know that there is in his own body a circulation in conformity with the law. I have furnished this picture in order to enlighten companions in search of the goal. When these two paths (the functioning and the control-ling) can be brought into unbroken connection, then all energy-paths are joined. The deer sleeps with his nose on his tail in order to close his controlling energy-path. The crane and the tortoise close their functioning-paths. Hence these three animals become at least a thousand years old. How much further can a man go! A man who carries on the cultivation of the Tao, who sets in motion the circulation in conformity with the law, in order to let consciousness and life circulate, need not fear that he is not lengthening his life and is not completing his path.

4. The Embryo of the Tao

According to the law, but without exertion, one must
    diligently fill oneself with light.

Forgetting appearance, look within and help the true
  spiritual power!
Ten months the embryo is under fire.
After a year the washings and baths become warm.

The picture that belongs here corresponds to the one shown on
page 37.[1]

This picture will be found in the original edition of the
Leng-yen-ching. But the ignorant monks who did not recognize
the hidden meaning and knew nothing about the embryo of
the Tao have for this reason made the mistake of leaving this
picture out. I only found out through the explanations of
adepts that the Julai (Tathagata) knows real work on the
embryo of the Tao. This embryo is nothing corporeally
visible which might be completed by other beings, but is in
reality the spiritual breath-energy of the ego. First the spirit
must penetrate the breath-energy (the soul), then the breath-
energy envelops the spirit. When spirit and breath-energy are
firmly united and the thoughts quiet and immobile, this is
described as the embryo. The breath-energy must crystallize;
only then will the spirit become effective. Therefore it is said
in the *Leng-yen-ching*: 'Take maternal care of the awakening
and the answering.' The two energies nourish and strengthen
one another. Therefore it is said: 'Daily growth takes place.'
When the energy is strong enough and the embryo is round
and complete it comes out of the top of the head. This is what
is called: the completed appearance which comes forth as
embryo and begets itself as the son of the Buddha.

5. THE BIRTH OF THE FRUIT

Outside the body there is a body called the Buddha
  image.

[1] This explanatory note and the four similar ones that follow were
furnished by Hellmut Wilhelm. (C. F. B.)

The thought which is powerful, the absence of
  thoughts, is Bodhi.
The · thousand-petalled lotus flower opens, transformed through breath-energy.
Because of the crystallization of the spirit, a hundredfold splendour shines forth.

The picture that belongs here corresponds to the one shown on
page 47.

In the *Leng-yen-chou*[1] it is said: 'At that time the ruler of the
world caused a hundredfold precious light to beam from his
hair knots. In the midst of the light shone the thousand-
petalled, precious lotus flower. And there within the flower
sat a transformed Julai. And from the top of his head went ten
rays of white, precious light, which were visible everywhere.
The crowd looked up to the out-streaming light and the Julai
announced: "The divine, magic mantra is the appearance of the
light-spirit, therefore his name is Son of Buddha."'

If a man does not receive the teaching about consciousness·
and life, but merely repeats meditation formulae stolidly and
in solitude, how could there develop out of his own body the
Julai, who sits and shines forth in the lotus flower and appears
in his own spirit-body! Many say that the light-spirit is a
minor teaching; but how can that which a man receives from
the ruler of the world be a minor teaching? Herewith I have
betrayed the deepest secret of the *Leng-yen* in order to teach
disciples. He who receives this way rises at once to the dark
secret and no longer becomes submerged in the dust of every-
day life.

6. CONCERNING THE RETENTION OF THE TRANSFORMED BODY

Every separate thought takes shape and becomes
  visible in colour and form.

[1] *Suramgama* mantra. (H. W.)

The total spiritual power unfolds its traces and transforms itself into emptiness.
Going out into being and going into non-being, one
completes the miraculous Tao.
All separate shapes appear as bodies, united with a
true source.

The picture that belongs here corresponds to the one shown on
page 57.

7. THE FACE TURNED TO THE WALL

The shapes formed by the spirit-fire are only empty
colours and forms.
The light of human nature [*hsing*] shines back on the
primordial, the true.
The imprint of the heart floats in space; untarnished,
the moonlight shines.
The boat of life has reached the shore; bright shines
the sunlight.

The picture that belongs here corresponds to the one shown on
page 27.

8. EMPTY INFINITY

Without beginning, without end,
Without past, without future.
A halo of light surrounds the world of the law.
We forget one another, quiet and pure, altogether
powerful and empty.
The emptiness is irradiated by the light of the heart
and of heaven.
The water of the sea is smooth and mirrors the moon
in its surface.

77

The clouds disappear in blue space; the mountains
shine clear.

Consciousness reverts to contemplation; the moon-
disk rests alone.

The picture that belongs here is the one below.

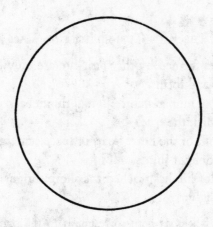

COMMENTARY

BY

C. G. JUNG

INTRODUCTION

I. DIFFICULTIES ENCOUNTERED BY A EUROPEAN IN TRYING TO UNDERSTAND THE EAST

A THOROUGH WESTERNER in feeling, I am necessarily deeply impressed by the strangeness of this Chinese text. It is true that some knowledge of Eastern religions and philosophies aids my intellect and intuition in understanding these ideas to a certain extent, just as I can understand the paradoxes of primitive beliefs in terms of 'ethnology', or in terms of the 'comparative history of religions'. Indeed, this is the Western way of hiding one's heart under the cloak of so-called scientific understanding. We do it partly because of the *misérable vanité des savants* which fears and rejects with horror any sign of living sympathy, and partly because a sympathetic understanding might permit contact with an alien spirit to become a serious experience. So-called scientific objectivity would have reserved this text for the philological acuity of Sinologues, and would have guarded it jealously from any other interpretation. But Richard Wilhelm penetrated into the secret and mysterious vitality of Chinese wisdom too deeply to have allowed such a pearl of intuitive insight to disappear in the pigeonholes of the specialists. I am greatly honoured that his choice of a psychological commentator has fallen upon me.

This entails the risk, though, that this unique treasure will be swallowed by still another special science. None the less, anyone seeking to minimize the merits of Western science and scholarship is undermining the main support of the European mind. Science is not, indeed, a perfect instrument, but it is a superior and indispensable one that works harm only when taken as an end in itself. Scientific method must serve; it errs when it usurps a throne. It must be ready to serve all branches of science, because each, by reason of its insufficiency, has need of support from the others. Science is the tool of the Western mind and with it more doors can be opened than with bare hands. It is part and parcel of our knowledge and obscures our insight only when it holds that the understanding given by it is the only kind there is. The East has taught us another, wider, more profound, and higher understanding, that is, understanding through life. We know this way only vaguely, as a mere shadowy sentiment culled from religious terminology, and therefore we gladly dispose of Eastern 'wisdom' in quotation marks, and relegate it to the obscure territory of faith and superstition. But in this way we wholly misunderstand the 'realism' of the East. This text, for instance, does not consist of exaggerated sentiment or overwrought mystical intuitions bordering on the pathological and emanating from ascetic cranks and recluses. It is based on the practical insights of highly evolved Chinese minds, which we have not the slightest justification for undervaluing.

This assertion may seem bold, perhaps, and is likely to be met with disbelief, but that is not surprising, considering how little is known about the material. Moreover, the strangeness of the material is so arresting that our embarrassment as to how and where the Chinese world of thought might be joined to ours is quite understandable. When faced with this problem of grasping the ideas of the East, the usual mistake of Western man is like that of the student in *Faust*. Misled by the Devil, he contemptuously turns his back on science, and, carried away by Eastern occultism, takes over yoga practices quite literally and becomes a pitiable imitator. (Theosophy is our best example of this mistake.) And so he abandons the one safe foundation of the Western mind and loses himself in a mist of words and ideas which never would have originated in European brains, and which can never be profitably grafted upon them.

An ancient adept has said: 'If the wrong man uses the right means, the right means work in the wrong way.' This Chinese saying, unfortunately all too true, stands in sharp contrast to our belief in the 'right' method irrespective of the man who applies it. In reality, in such matters everything depends on the man and little or nothing on the method. For the method is merely the path, the direction taken by a man. The way he acts is the true expression of his nature. If it ceases to be this, then the method is nothing more than an affectation, something artificially added, rootless and sapless, serving only the illegitimate goal of self-deception. It becomes a means of fooling oneself and of evading what may perhaps be the implacable law of one's being. This is far removed from the earth-born quality and sincerity of Chinese thought. On the contrary, it is the denial of one's own being, self-betrayal to strange and unclean gods, a cowardly trick for the purpose of usurping psychic superiority, everything in fact which is profoundly contrary to the meaning of the Chinese 'method'. For these insights result from a way of life that is complete, genuine, and true in the fullest sense; they are insights coming from that ancient, cultural life of China which has grown consistently and coherently from the deepest instincts, and which, for us, is forever remote and impossible to imitate.

Western imitation of the East is doubly tragic in that it comes from an unpsychological misunderstanding as sterile as are the modern escapades in Taos, the blissful South Sea Islands, and Central Africa, where 'primitivity' is earnestly being played at while Western civilized man evades his menacing duties, his *Hic Rhodus hic salta*. It is not a question of our imitating, or worse still, becoming missionaries for what is organically foreign, but rather a question of building up our own Western culture, which sickens with a thousand ills. This has to be done on the spot, and by the real European as he is in his Western commonplaces, with his marriage problems, his neuroses, his social and political delusions, and his whole philosophical disorientation.

We should do well to confess at once that, fundamentally speaking, we do not understand the complete detachment from the world of a text like this, indeed, that we do not want to understand it. Have we, perhaps, an inkling that a mental attitude which can direct the glance inward to this extent can bring about such detachment only because these people have so completely fulfilled the instinctive demands of their natures that little or nothing prevents them from viewing the invisible essence of the world? Can it be, perhaps, that the premise of such vision is liberation from those ambitions and passions which bind us to the visible world, and does not this liberation result from the sensible fulfilment of instinctive demands, rather than from the premature or fear-born repression of them? Is it that our eyes are opened to the spirit only when the laws of earth are obeyed? Anybody who knows the history of Chinese culture, and has also carefully studied the *I Ching*, that book of wisdom which for thousands of years has permeated all Chinese thought, will not pass over these questions lightly. He will know, moreover, that the views set forth in our text are nothing extraordinary from the Chinese point of view, but are actually inescapable, psychological conclusions.

In our Christian culture, spirit, and the passion of the spirit, were for a long time the greatest values and the things most worth striving for. Only after the decline of the Middle Ages, that is, in the course of the nineteenth century, when spirit began to degenerate into intellect, did a reaction set in against the unbearable dominance of intellectualism. This movement, it is true, at first committed the pardonable mistake of confusing intellect with spirit, and blaming the latter for the misdeeds of the former. Intellect does, in fact, harm the soul when it dares to possess itself of the heritage of the spirit. It is in no way fitted to do this, because spirit is something higher than intellect in that it includes not only the latter, but the feelings as well. It is a direction, or principle, of life that strives towards shining, supra-human heights. In opposition to it stands the dark, the feminine, the earth-bound principle (yin), with its emotionality and instinctiveness that reach far back into the depths of time, and into the roots of physiological continuity. Without a doubt, these concepts are purely intuitive insights, but one cannot very well dispense with them if one is trying to understand the nature of the human soul. China could not do without them because, as the history of Chinese philosophy shows, it has never gone so far from central psychic facts as to lose itself in a one-sided over-development and over-valuation of a single psychic function. Therefore, the Chinese have never failed to recognize the paradoxes and the polarity inherent in what is alive. The opposites always balanced one another—a sign of high culture. One-sidedness, though it lends momentum, is a mark of barbarism. The reaction which is now beginning in the West against the intellect in favour of feeling, or in favour of intuition, seems to me a mark of cultural advance, a widening of consciousness beyond the too narrow limits of a tyrannical intellect.

I have no wish to under-value the tremendous differentiation of Western intellect; measured by it, Eastern intellect can be described as childish. (Obviously this has nothing to do with intelligence.) If we should succeed in elevating another, or even a third psychic function to the dignity accorded intellect, then the West might expect to surpass the East by a very great margin. Therefore it is sad indeed when the European departs from his own nature and imitates the East or 'affects' it in any way. The possibilities open to him would be so much greater if he would remain true to himself and develop out of his own nature all that the East has brought forth from its inner being in the course of the centuries.

In general, and looked at from the incurably external point of view of the intellect, it would seem as if the things so highly valued by the East were not desirable for us. Intellect alone cannot fathom at first the practical importance Eastern ideas might have for us, and that is why it can classify these ideas as philosophical and ethnological curiosities and nothing more. The lack of comprehension goes so far that even learned Sinologues have not understood the practical application of the *I Ching*, and have therefore looked on the book as a collection of abstruse magic spells.

2. MODERN PSYCHOLOGY OFFERS A POSSIBILITY OF UNDERSTANDING

Observations made in my practice have opened to me a quite new and unexpected approach to Eastern wisdom. But it must be well understood that I did not have a knowledge, however inadequate, of Chinese philosophy as a starting point. On the contrary, when I began my life-work in the practice of psychiatry and psychotherapy, I was completely ignorant of Chinese philosophy, and only later did my professional experience show me that in my technique I had been unconsciously led along that secret way which has been the preoccupation of the best minds of the East for centuries. This could be taken for a subjective fancy—one reason for my previous reluctance to publish anything on the subject—but Richard Wilhelm, that great interpreter of the soul of China, fully confirmed the parallel for me. Thus he gave me the courage to write about a Chinese text which belongs entirely to the mysterious shadows of the Eastern mind. At the same time, and this is the extraordinary thing, in content it is a living parallel to what takes place in the psychic development of my patients, none of whom is Chinese.

In order to make this strange fact more intelligible to the reader, it must be pointed out that just as the human body shows a common anatomy over and above all racial differences, so, too, the psyche possesses a common substratum transcending all differences in culture and consciousness. I have called this substratum the collective unconscious. This unconscious psyche, common to all mankind, does not consist merely of contents capable of becoming conscious, but of latent dispositions towards certain identical reactions. Thus the fact of the collective unconscious is simply the psychic expression of the identity of brain-structure irrespective of all racial differences. This explains the analogy, sometimes even identity, between various myth-motifs, and symbols, and the possibility of human beings making themselves mutually understood. The various lines of psychic development start from one common stock whose roots reach back into all the strata of the past. This also explains the psychological parallelisms with animals.

Taken purely psychologically, it means that mankind has common instincts of imagination and of action. All conscious imagination and action have been developed with these unconscious archetypal images as their basis, and always remain bound up with them. Especially is this the case when consciousness has not attained any high degree of clarity, that is, when, in all its functions, it is more dependent on the instincts than on the conscious will, more governed by affect than by rational judgement. This condition ensures a primitive health of the psyche, which, however, immediately becomes lack of adaptation as soon as circumstances arise calling for a higher moral effort. Instincts suffice only for the individual embedded in nature, which, on the whole, remains always the same. An individual who is more guided by unconscious than by conscious choice tends therefore towards marked psychic conservatism. This is the reason the primitive does not change in the course of thousands of years, and it is also the reason why he fears everything strange and unusual. It might lead him to maladaptation, and thus to the greatest of psychic dangers, to a kind of neurosis in fact. A higher and wider consciousness, which comes about only through assimilation of the unfamiliar, tends towards autonomy, towards revolution against the old gods who are nothing other than those powerful, unconscious, archetypal images which have always held consciousness in thrall.

The more powerful and independent consciousness, and with it the conscious will, become, the more the unconscious is forced into the background. When this happens, it is easily possible for the conscious structures to detach themselves from the unconscious archetypes. Gaining thus in freedom, they break the chains of mere instinctiveness, and finally arrive at a state that is deprived of, or contrary to, instinct. Consciousness thus is torn from its roots and no longer able to appeal to the authority of the archetypal images; it has Promethean freedom, it is true, but also a godless *hybris*. It does indeed soar above the earth, even above mankind, but the danger of an upset is there, not for every individual, to be sure, but collectively for the weak members of such a society, who then, again like Prometheus, are chained to the Caucasus by the unconscious. The wise Chinese would say in the words of the *I Ching*: When yang has reached its greatest strength, the dark power of yin is born within its depths, for night begins at midday when yang breaks up and begins to change to yin.

A physician is in a position to see this peripeteia enacted literally in life. He sees, for instance, a successful businessman attaining all his desires heedless of his peril, and then, having withdrawn from activity at the height of his success, falling in a short time into a neurosis, which changes him into a querulous old woman, fastens him to his bed, and thus finally destroys him. The picture is complete even to the change from a masculine to a womanish attitude. An exact parallel to this is the legend of Nebuchadnezzar in the Book of Daniel, and indeed, Caesarean madness in general. Similar cases of one-sided exaggeration in the conscious standpoint, and of the corresponding yin reaction of the unconscious, form no small part of the practice of psychiatrists in our time, which so over-values the conscious will as to believe that 'where there is a will there is a way'. Not that I wish to detract in the least from the high moral value of conscious willing; consciousness and will may well continue to be considered the highest cultural achievements of humanity. But of what use is a morality that destroys the human being? To bring will and capacity into harmony seems to me to be a better thing than morality. Morality *à tout prix* is a sign of barbarism—more often wisdom is better—but perhaps I look at this through the professional glasses of the physician who has to mend the ills following in the wake of an exaggerated cultural achievement.

Be that as it may. In any case, it is a fact that consciousness heightened by a necessary one-sidedness gets so far out of touch with the archetypes that a breakdown follows. Long before the actual catastrophe, the signs of error announce themselves as absence of instinct, nervousness, disorientation, and entanglement in impossible situations and problems. When the physician comes to investigate, he finds an unconscious which is in complete rebellion against the values of the conscious, and which therefore cannot possibly be assimilated to the conscious, while the reverse, of course, is altogether out of the question. We are then confronted with an apparently irreconcilable conflict with which human reason cannot deal except by sham solutions or dubious compromises. If both these evasions are rejected, we are faced with the question as to what has become of the much needed unity of personality, and with the necessity of seeking it. And here we come to the path travelled by the East from time immemorial. Quite obviously, the Chinese owes the finding of this path to the fact that he was never able to force the opposites in human nature so far apart that all conscious connection between them was lost. The Chinese has such an all-inclusive consciousness because, as in the case of primitive mentality, the yea and the nay have remained in their original proximity. None the less, he could not escape feeling the collision of the opposites, and therefore he sought out that way of life in which he would be what the Hindu terms *nirdvandva*, free of the opposites.

Our text is concerned with this way, and this same problem comes up with my patients also. There could be no greater mistake than for a Westerner to take up the direct practice of Chinese yoga, for it would be a matter of his will and his consciousness, and would only strengthen the latter against the unconscious, bringing about the very effect to be avoided. The neurosis would then simply be intensified. It cannot be sufficiently strongly emphasized that we are not Orientals, and therefore have an entirely different point of departure in these things. It would also be a great mistake to assume that this is the path every neurotic must travel, or that it is the solution to be sought at every stage of the neurotic problem. It is appropriate only in those cases where the conscious has reached an abnormal degree of development, and has therefore diverged too far from the unconscious. This high degree of consciousness is the *conditio sine qua non*. Nothing would be more wrong than to wish to open this way to neurotics who are ill on account of an undue predominance of the unconscious. For the same reason, this way of development has scarcely any meaning before the middle of life (normally between the ages of thirty-five and forty); in fact, if entered upon too soon, it can be decidedly injurious.

As has been indicated, the reason for looking for a new way

was the fact that the fundamental problem of the patient seemed insoluble to me unless violence was done to the one or the other side of his nature. I always worked with the temperamental conviction that fundamentally there are no insoluble problems, and experience justified me in so far as I have often seen individuals simply outgrow a problem which had destroyed others. This 'outgrowing', as I formerly called it, on further experience was seen to consist in a new level of consciousness. Some higher or wider interest arose on the person's horizon, and through this widening of his view the insoluble problem lost its urgency. It was not solved logically in its own terms, but faded out when confronted with a new and stronger life-tendency. It was not repressed and made unconscious, but merely appeared in a different light, and so did indeed become different. What, on a lower level, had led to the wildest conflicts and to panicky outbursts of emotion, viewed from the higher level of the personality, now seemed like a storm in the valley seen from a high mountain-top. This does not mean that the thunderstorm is robbed of its reality, but instead of being in it, one is now above it. However, since we are both valley and mountain with respect to the psyche, it might seem a vain illusion to feel oneself beyond what is human. One certainly does feel the affect and is shaken and tormented by it, yet at the same time one is aware of a higher consciousness, which prevents one from becoming identical with the affect, a consciousness which takes the affect objectively, and can say, 'I know that I suffer.' What our text says of indolence: 'Indolence of which a man is conscious and indolence of which he is unconscious are a thousand miles apart', holds true in the highest degree of affect also.

Here and there it happened in my practice that a patient grew beyond himself because of unknown potentialities, and this became an experience of prime importance to me. I had learned in the meanwhile that the greatest and most important problems of life are all in a certain sense insoluble. They must be so because they express the necessary polarity inherent in every self-regulating system. They can never be solved, but only outgrown. I therefore asked myself whether this possibility of outgrowing, that is, further psychic development, was not the normal thing, and therefore remaining stuck in a conflict was what was pathological. Everyone must possess that higher level, at least in embryonic form, and in favourable circumstances must be able to develop this possibility. When I examined the way of development of those persons who quietly and, as if unconsciously, grew beyond themselves, I saw that their fates had something in common. The new thing came to them out of obscure possibilities either outside or inside themselves; they accepted it and developed further by means of it. It seemed to me typical that some took the new thing from outside themselves, others from within; or rather, that it grew into some persons from without, and into others from within. But the new thing never came exclusively either from within or from without. If it arose from outside, it became a deeply subjective experience; if it arose from within, it became an outer event. In no case was it conjured into existence through purpose and conscious willing, but rather seemed to be borne on the stream of time.

We are so greatly tempted to turn everything into purpose and method that I deliberately express myself in very abstract terms in order to avoid causing a prejudice in one direction or another. The new thing must not be pigeonholed under any heading, for then it becomes a recipe to be applied mechanically and it would again be a case of the 'right means' in the hands 'of the wrong man'. I have been deeply impressed with the fact that the new thing presented by fate seldom or never corresponds to conscious expectation. And still more remarkable, though the new thing contradicts deeply rooted instincts as we have known them, it is a singularly appropriate expression of the total personality, an expression which one could not imagine in a more complete form.

What did these people do in order to achieve the development that liberated them? As far as I could see they did nothing (*wu wei*)[1] but let things happen. As Master Lü-tsu teaches in our text, the light rotates according to its own law, if one does not give up one's ordinary occupation. The art of letting things happen, action through non-action, letting go of oneself, as taught by Meister Eckhart, became for me the key opening the door to the way. We must be able to let things happen in the psyche. For us, this actually is an art of which few people know anything. Consciousness is forever interfering, helping, correcting, and negating, and never leaving the simple growth of the psychic processes in peace. It would be simple enough, if only simplicity were not the most difficult of all things. To begin with, the task consists solely in objectively observing a ⸢ragment of a fantasy in its development. Nothing could be ،impler, and yet right here the difficulties begin. No fantasy-fragment seems to appear—or yes, one does—but it is too stupid—hundreds of good reasons inhibit it. One cannot concentrate on it—it is too boring—what would it amount to—it is 'nothing but', et cetera. The conscious mind raises prolific objections, in fact it often seems bent upon blotting out the spontaneous fantasy-activity in spite of real insight, even of firm determination on the part of the individual to allow the psychic processes to go forward without interference. Often a veritable cramp of consciousness exists.

If one is successful in overcoming the initial difficulties, ciriticism is still likely to start in afterwards and attempt to interpret the fantasy, to classify, to aestheticize, or to depreciate it. The temptation to do this is almost irresistible. After complete and faithful observation, free rein can be given to the impatience of the conscious mind; in fact it must be given, else

[1] Action through non-action. (C. F. B.)

obstructing resistances develop. But each time the fantasy material is to be produced, the activity of consciousness must again be put aside.

In most cases the results of these efforts are not very encouraging at first. They usually consist of webs of fantasy which yield no clear knowledge of their origin or goal. Also, the way of getting at the fantasies is individually different. For many people, it is easiest to write them; others visualize them, and others again draw and paint them with or without visualization. In cases of a high degree of conscious cramp, oftentimes the hands alone can fantasy; they model or draw figures that are often quite foreign to the conscious mind.

These exercises must be continued until the cramp in the conscious mind is released, or, in other words, until one can let things happen, which was the immediate goal of the exercise. In this way a new attitude is created, an attitude which accepts the non-rational and the incomprehensible, simply because it is what is happening. This attitude would be poison for a person who had already been overwhelmed by things that just happen, but it is of the highest value for one who chooses, with an exclusively conscious critique, only the things acceptable to his consciousness from among the things that happen, and thus is gradually drawn out of the stream of life into stagnant backwater.

At this point, the way travelled by the two types mentioned above seems to be separate. Both have learned to accept what comes to them. (As Master Lü-tsu teaches: 'When occupations come to us we must accept them; when things come to us we must understand them from the ground up.') One man will chiefly take what comes to him from without, and the other what comes from within, and, according to the law of life, the one will have to take from the outside something he never could accept before from outside, and the other will accept from within things which would always have been excluded before.

This reversal of one's being means an enlargement, heightening, and enrichment of the personality when the previous values are retained along with the change, provided, of course, that these values are not mere illusions. If the values are not retained, the individual goes over to the other side, and passes from fitness to unfitness, from adaptation to the lack of it, from sense to nonsense, and even from rationality to mental disturbance. The way is not without danger. Everything good is costly, and the development of the personality is one of the most costly of all things. It is a question of yea-saying to oneself, of taking one's self as the most serious of tasks, of being conscious of everything one does, and keeping it constantly before one's eyes in all its dubious aspects—truly a task that taxes us to the utmost.

The Chinese can fall back upon the authority of his entire culture. If he starts on the long way, he does what is recognized as being the best of all the things he could do. But the Westerner who wishes to start upon this way, if he is truly serious about it, has all authority against him—intellectual, moral, and religious. That is why it is infinitely easier for a man to imitate the Chinese way, and desert the troublesome European, or else to seek again the way back to the medievalism of the Christian Church, and build up once more the European wall intended to separate true Christians from the poor heathen and the ethnographic curiosities dwelling outside. Aesthetic or intellectual flirtations with life and fate come to an abrupt end here. The step to higher consciousness leads us out and away from all rear-guard cover and from all safety measures. The individual must give himself to the new way completely, for it is only by means of his integrity that he can go further, and only his integrity can guarantee that his way does not turn out to be an absurd adventure.

Whether a person's fate comes to him from without or from within, the experiences and events of the way remain the same.

Therefore I need say nothing about the manifold outer and inner events, the endless variety of which I could never exhaust in any case. To do so, moreover, would be irrelevant to the text under discussion. But there is much to be said of the psychic states that accompany the further development. These psychic states are expressed symbolically in our text, and in the very symbols which for many years have been familiar to me in my practice.

THE FUNDAMENTAL CONCEPTS

I. THE TAO

THE GREAT DIFFICULTY in interpreting this and similar texts[1] for the European mind is due to the fact that the Chinese author always starts from the central point, from the point we would call his objective or goal; in a word, he begins with the ultimate insight he has set out to attain. Thus the Chinese author begins his work with ideas that demand such a comprehensive understanding that a person of discriminating mind must feel that he would be guilty of ridiculous pretension, or even of talking utter nonsense, if he should embark on an intellectual discourse on the subtle psychic experiences of the greatest minds of the East. For example, our text begins: 'That which exists through itself is called the Way.' The *Hui Ming Ching* begins with the words: 'The subtlest secret of the Tao is human nature and life.'

It is characteristic of the Western mind that it has no concept for Tao. The Chinese character is made up of the character for 'head', and that for 'going'. Wilhelm translates Tao by *Sinn* (Meaning).[2] Others translate it as 'way', 'providence', or even as 'God', as the Jesuits do. This shows the difficulty. 'Head' can be taken as consciousness,[3] and 'to go' as travelling a way, thus the idea would be: to go consciously, or the conscious way. This agrees with the fact that 'the light of heaven' which

---

[1] Compare *Hui Ming Ching*, p. 69.
[2] Also as the Way; see p. 11. (C. F. B.)
[3] The head is also the 'seat of heavenly light'.

'dwells between the eyes' as the 'heart of heaven' is used synonymously with Tao. Human nature and life are contained in 'the light of heaven' and, according to Liu Hua-yang, are the most important secrets of the Tao. Now 'light' is the symbolical equivalent of consciousness, and the nature of consciousness is expressed by analogies with light. The *Hui Ming Ching* is introduced with the verse:

> If thou wouldst complete the diamond body with no
> outflowing,
> Diligently heat the roots of consciousness[1] and life.
> Kindle light in the blessed country ever close at hand,
> And there hidden, let thy true self always dwell.

These verses contain a sort of alchemistic instruction, a method or way of creating the 'diamond body' which is also meant in our text. 'Heating' is necessary; that is, there must be an intensification of consciousness in order that the dwelling place of the spirit may be 'illumined'. But not only consciousness, life itself must be intensified. The union of these two produces 'conscious life'. According to the *Hui Ming Ching*, the ancient sages knew how to bridge the gap between consciousness and life because they cultivated both. In this way the *sheli*, the immortal body, is 'melted out', and in this way 'the great Tao is completed'.[2]

If we take the Tao to be the method or conscious way by which to unite what is separated, we have probably come close to the psychological content of the concept. In any case, the separation of consciousness from life cannot very well be understood to mean anything but what I have described above as an aberration, or deracination, of consciousness. Without doubt, also, the realization of the opposite hidden in the uncon-

---

[1] In the *Hui Ming Ching*, 'human nature' [*hsing*] and 'consciousness' [*hui*] are used interchangeably. (Both are opposites to life [*ming*] but are not identical with each other. C. F. B.)

[2] P. 70.

scious, i.e. the 'reversal', signifies reunion with the unconscious laws of being, and the purpose of this reunion is the attainment of conscious life or, expressed in Chinese terms, the bringing about of the Tao.

2. THE CIRCULAR MOVEMENT AND THE CENTRE

As has already been pointed out, the union of opposites[1] on a higher level of consciousness is not a rational thing, nor is it a matter of will; it is a psychic process of development which expresses itself in symbols. Historically, this process has always been represented in symbols, and to-day the development of individual personality still presents itself in symbolical figures. This fact was revealed to me in the following observations. The spontaneous fantasy products we mentioned above become more profound and concentrate themselves gradually around abstract structures which apparently represent 'principles', true Gnostic *archai*. When the fantasies are chiefly expressed in thoughts, the results are intuitive formulations of dimly felt laws or principles, which at first tend to be dramatized or personified. (We shall come back to these again later.) If the fantasies are expressed in drawings, symbols appear which are chiefly of the so-called mandala[2] type. 'Mandala' means a circle, more especially a magic circle, and this symbol is not only to be found all through the East but also among us; mandalas are amply represented in the Middle Ages. The early Middle Ages are especially rich in Christian mandalas, and for the most part show Christ in the centre, with the four evangelists, or their symbols, at the cardinal points. This conception

[1] Compare my discussion in *Psychological Types*, chapter v [London and New York, 1923].

[2] For a discussion of the mandala, see Heinrich Zimmer, *Kunstform und Yoga im Indischen Kultbild*, Frankfurter-Verlaganstalt, Berlin, 1926; Mircea Eliade, *Yoga: Immortality and Freedom*, Bollingen Series LVI, London and New York, 1958. (C. F. B.)

must be a very ancient one, for the Egyptians[1] represented Horus with his four sons in the same way. (It is known that Horus with his four sons has close connections with Christ and the four evangelists.) Later there is to be found an unmistakable and very interesting mandala in Jacob Boehme's book on the soul.[2] This latter mandala, it is clear, deals with a psycho-cosmic system strongly coloured by Christian ideas. Boehme calls it the 'philosophical eye',[3] or the 'mirror of wisdom', which obviously means a *summa* of secret knowledge. For the most part, the mandala form is that of a flower, cross, or wheel, with a distinct tendency towards quadripartite structure. (One is reminded of the *tetraktys*, the fundamental number in the Pythagorean system.) Mandalas of this sort are also to be found in the sand paintings used in the ceremonies of the Pueblo and Navaho Indians.[4] But the most beautiful mandalas are, of course, those of the East, especially those belonging to Tibetan Buddhism. The symbols of our text are represented in these mandalas. I have also found mandala drawings among the mentally ill, and indeed among persons who certainly did not have the least idea of any of the connections we have discussed.[5]

Among my patients I have come across cases of women who did not draw mandalas but who danced them instead. In India this type is called *mandala nrithya* or mandala dance, and the dance figures express the same meanings as the drawings. My patients can say very little about the meaning of the symbols but are fascinated by them and find them in some way or

[1] Compare Wallis Budge, *The Gods of the Egyptians*, London, 1904.

[2] *For the Questions of the Soule*, 1602, first English translation.

[3] Compare the Chinese concept of the heavenly light between the eyes.

[4] Matthews, *The Mountain Chant*, Fifth Annual Report of the Bureau of Ethnology, 1883-4, and Stevenson, *Ceremonial of Hasjelti Dailjiis*, Eighth Annual Report of the Bureau of Ethnology, 1886-7.

[5] I have published the mandala of a somnambulist in *Collected Papers on Analytical Psychology*. (For the revised version of this essay, see *Psychiatric Studies*, vol. 1 of Jung's Collected Works, translated by R. F. C. Hull. Bollingen Series XX, London and New York, 1957. C. F. B.)

other expressive and effective with respect to their psychic condition.

Our text promises to 'reveal the secret of the Golden Flower of the great One'. The Golden Flower is the light, and the light of heaven is the Tao. The Golden Flower is a mandala symbol which I have often met with in the material brought me by my patients. It is drawn either seen from above as a regular geometric ornament, or as a blossom growing from a plant. The plant is frequently a structure in brilliant fiery colours growing out of a bed of darkness, and carrying the blossom of light at the top, a symbol similar to that of the Christmas tree. A drawing of this kind also expresses the origin of the Golden Flower, for according to the *Hui Ming Ching* the 'germinal vesicle' is nothing other than the 'yellow castle', the 'heavenly heart', the 'terrace of life', the 'square inch field of the square foot house', the 'purple hall of the city of jade', the 'dark pass', the 'space of former heaven', the 'dragon castle at the bottom of the sea'. It is also called the 'border region of the snow mountains', the 'primal pass', the 'realm of the greatest joy', the 'land without boundaries', and 'the altar upon which consciousness and life are made'. 'If a dying man does not know this germinal vesicle,' says the *Hui Ming Ching*, 'he will not find the unity of consciousness and life in a thousand births, nor in ten thousand aeons.'

The beginning, in which everything is still one, and which therefore appears as the highest goal, lies at the bottom of the sea in the darkness of the unconscious. In the germinal vesicle, consciousness and life ('human nature' and 'life', *hsing-ming*) are still a 'unity',[1] 'inseparably mixed like the sparks in the refining furnace'. 'Within the germinal vesicle is the fire of the ruler.' '. . . all the sages began their work at the germinal vesicle.' Note the fire analogies. I know a series of European mandala drawings in which something like a plant seed surrounded by

[1] *Hui Ming Ching*, p. 70.

its coverings is shown floating in water, and from the depths below, fire penetrating the seed makes it grow and causes the formation of a large golden flower from within the germinal vesicle.

This symbolism refers to a sort of alchemical process of refining and ennobling; darkness gives birth to light; out of the 'lead of the water-region' grows the noble gold; what is unconscious becomes conscious in the form of a process of life and growth. (Hindu Kundalini yoga[1] affords a complete analogy.) In this way the union of consciousness and life takes place.

When my patients produce these mandala pictures it is, of course, not through suggestion; similar pictures were being made long before I knew their meaning or their connection with the practices of the East, which, at that time, were wholly unfamiliar to me. The pictures came quite spontaneously and from two sources. One source is the unconscious, which spontaneously produces such fantasies; the other source is life, which, if lived with complete devotion, brings an intuition of the self, the individual being. Awareness of the individual self is expressed in the drawing, while the unconscious exacts devotedness to life. For quite in accord with the Eastern conception, the mandala symbol is not only a means of expression, but works an effect. It reacts upon its maker. Very ancient magical effects lie hidden in this symbol for it derives originally from the 'enclosing circle', the 'charmed circle', the magic of which has been preserved in countless folk customs.[2] The image has the obvious purpose of drawing a *sulcus primigenius*, a magical furrow around the centre, the *templum*, or *temenos* (sacred precinct), of the innermost personality, in order to prevent 'flowing out', or to guard by apo-

[1] A. Avalon, *The Serpent Power*, London, 1931.
[2] See the excellent collection of E. F. Knuchel, *Die Umwandlung in Kult, Magie und Rechtsgebrauch*, Basel, 1919.

tropaeic means against deflections through external influences. The magical practices are nothing but the projections of psychic events, which are here applied in reverse to the psyche, like a kind of spell on one's own personality. That is to say, by means of these concrete performances, the attention, or better said, the interest, is brought back to an inner, sacred domain, which is the source and goal of the soul and which contains the unity of life and consciousness. The unity once possessed has been lost, and must now be found again.

The unity of these two, life and consciousness, is the Tao, whose symbol would be the central white light (compare the Bardo Thödol, the Tibetan Book of the Dead).[1] This light dwells in the 'square inch', or in the 'face', that is, between the eyes. It is the image of the creative point, a point having intensity without extension, thought of as connected with the space of the 'square inch', the symbol for that which has extension. The two together make the Tao. Human nature [hsing] and consciousness [hui] are expressed in light symbolism, and are therefore intensity, while life [ming] would coincide with extensity. The first have the character of the yang principle, the latter of the yin. The above-mentioned mandala of a somnambulist girl, fifteen and a half years old, whom I had under observation thirty years ago, shows in its centre a 'spring of life-energy' without extension, which in its emanations collides directly with a contrary space-principle—a perfect analogy with the fundamental idea of the Chinese text.

The 'enclosure', or *circumambulatio*, is expressed in our text by the idea of a 'circulation'. The 'circulation' is not merely motion in a circle, but means, on the one hand, the marking off of the sacred precinct, and, on the other, fixation and concentration. The sun wheel begins to run; that is to say, the sun is animated and begins to take its course, or, in other words, the Tao begins to work and to take over the leadership. Action

[1] W. Y. Evans-Wentz, *The Tibetan Book of the Dead*, London, 1927.

is reversed into non-action; all that is peripheral is subjected to the command of what is central. Therefore it is said: 'Movement is only another name for mastery.' Psychologically, this circulation would be the 'turning in a circle around oneself', whereby, obviously, all sides of the personality become involved. 'They cause the poles of light and darkness to rotate,' that is, day and night alternate.

Es wechselt Paradieseshelle
Mit tiefer, schauervoller Nacht.[1]

Thus the circular movement also has the moral significance of activating all the light and the dark forces of human nature, and with them, all the psychological opposites of whatever kind they may be. It is self-knowledge by means of self-incubation (Sanskrit *tapas*). A similar archetypal concept of a perfect being is that of the Platonic man, round on all sides and uniting within himself the two sexes.

One of the finest parallels to what has been said here is the description of his central experience given by Edward Maitland, the collaborator of Anna Kingsford.[2] He had discovered that during reflection on an idea, related ideas became visible, so to speak, in a long series apparently reaching back to their source, which to him was the divine spirit. By means of concentration on this series, he tried to penetrate to their origin. He says: 'I was absolutely without knowledge or expectation when I yielded to the impulse to make the attempt. I simply experimented on a faculty . . . being seated at my writing-table the while in order to record the results as they came, and resolved to retain my hold on my outer and circumferential consciousness, no matter how far towards my inner and central

---

[1] 'The radiance of Paradise alternates with deep, dreadful night.' (*Faust*—C. F. B.)

[2] Edward Maitland, *Anna Kingsford, Her Life, Letters, Diary, and Work*, London, 1896. Cf. especially pages 129f. I am indebted for this reference to my esteemed colleague, Dr. Beatrice Hinkle, of New York.

consciousness I might go. For I knew not whether I should be able to regain the former if I once quitted my hold of it, or to recollect the facts of the experience. At length I achieved my object, though only by a strong effort, the tension occasioned by the endeavour to keep both extremes of the consciousness in view at once being very great.

'Once well started on my quest, I found myself traversing a succession of spheres or belts ... the impression produced being that of mounting a vast ladder stretching from the circumference towards the centre of a system, which was at once my own system, the solar system, and the universal system, the three systems being at once diverse and identical. ... Presently, by a supreme, and what I felt must be a final effort . . . I succeeded in polarizing the whole of the convergent rays of my consciousness into the desired focus. And at the same instant, as if through the sudden ignition of the rays thus fused into a unity, I found myself confronted with a glory of unspeakable whiteness and brightness, and of a lustre so intense as well-nigh to beat me back. . . . But though feeling that I had to explore further, I resolved to make assurance doubly sure by piercing if I could the almost blinding lustre, and seeing what it enshrined. With a great effort I succeeded, and the glance revealed to me that which I had felt must be there. . . . It was the dual form of the Son . . . the unmanifest made manifest, the unformulate formulate, the unindividuate individuate, God as the Lord, proving through His duality that God is Substance as well as Force, Love as well as Will, Feminine as well as Masculine, Mother as well as Father.' He found that God is two in one like man. Besides this he noticed something that our text also emphasizes, namely, 'suspension of breathing'. He says ordinary breathing stopped and was replaced by an internal respiration, 'as if by breathing of a distinct personality within and other than the physical organism'. He took this being to be the entelechy of Aristotle, and the inner Christ of the Apostle

Paul, the 'spiritual and substantial individuality engendered within the physical and phenomenal personality, and representing, therefore, the rebirth of man on a plane transcending the material'.

This genuine[1] experience contains all the essential symbols of our text. The phenomenon itself, that is, the vision of light, is an experience common to many mystics, and one that is undoubtedly of the greatest significance, because in all times and places it appears as the unconditional thing, which unites in itself the greatest energy and the profoundest meaning. Hildegarde of Bingen, an outstanding personality quite apart from her mysticism, expresses herself about her central vision in a similar way. 'Since my childhood,' she says, 'I have always seen a light in my soul, but not with the outer eyes, nor through the thoughts of my heart; neither do the five outer senses take part in this vision. . . . The light I perceive is not of a local kind, but is much brighter than the cloud which bears the sun. I cannot distinguish height, breadth, or length in it. . . . What I see or learn in such a vision stays long in my memory. I see, hear, and know in the same moment. . . . I cannot recognize any sort of form in this light, although I sometimes see in it another light that is known to me as the living light. . . . While I am enjoying the spectacle of this light, all sadness and sorrow vanish from my memory. . . .'

I know a few individuals who are familiar with this phenomenon from personal experience. As far as I have been able to understand it, the phenomenon seems to have to do with an acute state of consciousness, as intensive as it is abstract, a 'detached' consciousness (see below), which, as Hildegarde

---

[1] Such experiences are genuine, but their genuineness does not prove that all the conclusions or convictions forming their context are necessarily sound. Even in cases of lunacy one comes across perfectly valid psychic experiences.

(The above note was added by Jung to the first English translation.— C. F. B.)

pertinently remarks, brings up to consciousness regions of psychic events ordinarily covered with darkness. The fact that the general bodily sensations disappear during such an experience suggests that their specific energy has been withdrawn from them, and apparently gone towards heightening the clarity of consciousness. As a rule, the phenomenon is spontaneous, coming and going on its own initiative. Its effect is astonishing in that it almost always brings about a solution of psychic complications, and thereby frees the inner personality from emotional and intellectual entanglements, creating thus a unity of being which is universally felt as 'liberation'.

The conscious will cannot attain such a symbolic unity because the conscious is partisan in this case. Its opponent is the collective unconscious which does not understand the language of the conscious. Therefore it is necessary to have the magic of the symbol which contains those primitive analogies that speak to the unconscious. The unconscious can be reached and expressed only by symbols, which is the reason why the process of individuation can never do without the symbol. The symbol is the primitive expression of the unconscious, but at the same time it is also an idea corresponding to the highest intuition produced by consciousness.

The oldest mandala drawing known to me is a palaeolithic so-called 'sun wheel', recently discovered in Rhodesia. It also is based on the principle of four. Things reaching so far back in human history naturally touch upon the deepest layers of the unconscious and affect the latter where conscious speech shows itself to be quite impotent. Such things cannot be thought up but must grow again from the forgotten depths, if they are to express the deepest insights of consciousness and the loftiest intuitions of the spirit. Coming from these depths they blend together the uniqueness of present-day consciousness with the age-old past of life.

PHENOMENA OF THE WAY

1. THE DISINTEGRATION OF CONSCIOUSNESS

WHENEVER the narrowly delimited, but intensely clear, individual consciousness meets the immense expansion of the collective unconscious, there is danger because the latter has a definitely disintegrating effect on consciousness. Indeed, according to the exposition of the *Hui Ming Ching*, this effect belongs to the peculiar phenomena of Chinese yoga practice. It is said there[1]: 'Every separate thought takes shape and becomes visible in colour and form. The total spiritual power unfolds its traces. . . .'[2] One of the illustrations accompanying the book shows a sage sunk in contemplation, his head surrounded by tongues of fire, out of which five human figures emerge; these five split up again into twenty-five smaller figures. This would be a schizophrenic process if it were to become a permanent state. Therefore the instructions, as though warning the adept, say: 'The shapes formed by the spirit-fire are only empty colours and forms. / The light of human nature [*hsing*] shines back on the primordial, the true.'

Thus it is understandable that the text returns to the protecting figure of the 'enclosing circle'. It is intended to prevent 'outflowing' and to protect the unity of consciousness from being split apart by the unconscious. Moreover, the Chinese concept points a way towards lessening the disintegrating

---

[1] P. 76.

[2] Cf. the recurrent memories of earlier incarnations that arise during contemplation.

effect of the unconscious; it describes the 'thought-figures' or 'separate thoughts' as 'empty colours and shapes', and thus depotentiates them as much as possible. This idea runs through the whole of Buddhism (especially the Mahayana form), and, in the instructions to the dead in the Tibetan Book of the Dead, it is even pushed to the point of explaining favourable as well as unfavourable gods as illusions still to be overcome. It certainly is not within the competence of the psychologist to establish the metaphysical truth or falsity of this idea; he must be content to determine wherever possible what has psychic effect. In doing this, he need not bother himself as to whether the shape in question is a transcendental illusion or not, since faith, not science, has to decide this point. We are working here in a field which for a long time has seemed to be outside the domain of science, and which has therefore been looked upon as wholly illusory. But there is no scientific justification for such an assumption, for the substantiality of these things is not a scientific problem since in any case it would lie beyond the range of human perception and judgement, and therefore beyond any possibility of proof. The psychologist is not concerned with the substance of these complexes, but with the psychic experience. Without a doubt they are psychic contents which can be experienced, and which have an indisputable autonomy. They are fragmentary psychic systems which either appear spontaneously in ecstatic states and, under certain circumstances, elicit powerful impressions and effects, or else become fixed as mental disturbances in the form of delusions and hallucinations, thus destroying the unity of the personality.

The psychiatrist is prone to believe in toxins and the like, and to explain schizophrenia (splitting of the mind in a psychosis) in these terms, and hence to put no emphasis on the psychic contents. On the other hand, in psychogenic disturbances (hysteria, compulsion neurosis, etc.), where toxic effects and cell degeneration are out of the question, spontaneous split-off complexes are to be found, as, for example, in somnambulistic states. Freud, it is true, would like to explain these as due to unconscious repression of sexuality, but this explanation is by no means valid for all cases, because contents which the conscious cannot assimilate can evolve spontaneously out of the unconscious, and the repression hypothesis is inadequate in such instances. Moreover, the essential autonomy of these elements can be observed in the affects of daily life which obstinately obtrude themselves against our wills, and then, in spite of our earnest efforts to repress them, overwhelm the ego and force it under their control. No wonder that the primitive either sees in these moods a state of possession or sets them down to a loss of soul. Our colloquial speech reflects the same thing when we say: 'I don't know what has got into him to-day'; 'He is possessed of the devil'; 'He is beside himself'; 'He behaves as if possessed'. Even legal practice recognizes a degree of diminished responsibility in a state of affect. Autonomic psychic contents thus are quite common experiences for us. Such contents have a disintegrating effect on the conscious mood.

But besides the ordinary, familiar affects, there are subtler, more complex emotional states which can no longer be described as affects pure and simple but which are complicated fragmentary psychic systems. The more complicated they are, the more they have the character of personalities. As constituent factors of the psychic personality, they necessarily have the character of 'persons'. Such fragmentary systems appear especially in mental diseases, in cases of psychogenic splitting of the personality (double personality), and of course in mediumistic phenomena. They are also encountered in religious phenomena. Many of the earlier gods have evolved out of 'persons' into personified ideas, and finally into abstract ideas, for activated unconscious contents always appear first as projections upon the outside world. In the course of mental development, consciousness gradually assimilates them as projections in space and reshapes them into conscious ideas which then forfeit their originally autonomous and personal character. As we know, some of the old gods have become mere descriptive attributes via astrology (martial, jovial, saturnine, erotic, logical, lunatic, and so on).

The instructions of the Tibetan Book of the Dead in particular enable us to see how greatly the conscious is threatened with disintegration through these figures. Again and again, the dead are instructed not to take these shapes for truth, and not to confuse their murky appearance with the pure white light of *Dharmakaya* ('the divine body of truth'). The meaning is that they are not to project the one light of highest consciousness into concretized figures, and in such a way dissolve it into a plurality of autonomous fragmentary systems. If there were no danger of this, and if these systems did not represent menacingly autonomous and divergent tendencies, such urgent instructions would not be necessary. If we consider the simpler, polytheistically oriented attitude of the Eastern mind, these instructions would almost be the equivalent of warnings to a Christian not to let himself be blinded by the illusion of a personal God, not to mention a Trinity and innumerable angels and saints.

If tendencies towards disassociation were not inherent in the human psyche, parts never would have been split off; in other words, neither spirits nor gods would ever have come to exist. That is the reason, too, that our time is so utterly godless and profane, for we lack knowledge of the unconscious psyche and pursue the cult of consciousness to the exclusion of all else. Our true religion is a monotheism of consciousness, a possession by it, coupled with a fanatical denial that there are parts of the psyche which are autonomous. But we differ from the Buddhist yoga doctrine in that we even deny that such autonomous parts are experienceable. A great psychic danger arises here, because the parts then behave like any other repressed contents: they necessarily induce wrong attitudes, for the repressed material appears again in consciousness in a spurious form. This fact, which is so striking in every case of neurosis, holds true also for collective psychic phenomena. In this respect our time is caught in a fatal error: we believe we can criticize religious facts intellectually; we think, for instance, like Laplace, that God is a hypothesis which can be subjected to intellectual treatment, to affirmation or denial. It is completely forgotten that the reason mankind believes in the 'daemon' has nothing whatever to do with outside factors, but is due to simple perception of the powerful inner effect of the autonomous fragmentary systems. This effect is not nullified by criticizing its name intellectually, nor by describing it as false. The effect is collectively always present; the autonomous systems are always at work, because the fundamental structure of the unconscious is not touched by the fluctuations of a transitory consciousness.

If we deny the existence of the autonomous systems, imagining that we have got rid of them by a critique of the name, then their effect which nevertheless continues cannot be understood, and they can no longer be assimilated to consciousness. They become an inexplicable factor of disturbance which we finally assume must exist somewhere or other outside of ourselves. In this way, a projection of the autonomous fragmentary systems results, and at the same time a dangerous situation is created, because the disturbing effects are now attributed to bad will outside ourselves which of course is not to be found anywhere but at our neighbour's—*de l'autre côté de la rivière*. This leads to collective delusions, 'incidents', war, and revolution, in a word, to destructive mass psychoses.

Insanity is possession by an unconscious content which, as such, is not assimilated to consciousness; nor can it be assimilated, since the conscious mind has denied the existence of such contents. Expressed in terms of religion, the attitude is equivalent to saying: 'We no longer have any fear of God and believe that everything is to be judged by human standards.' This *hybris*, that is, this narrowness of consciousness, is always the shortest way to the insane asylum. I recommend the excellent presentation of this problem in H. G. Wells' novel *Christina Alberta's Father*, and Schreber's *Denkwürdigkeiten eines Nervenkranken*.[1]

The enlightened European is likely to be relieved when it is said in the *Hui Ming Ching* that the 'shapes formed by the spirit-fire are only empty colours and forms'. That sounds quite European and seems to suit our reason excellently. Indeed, we think we can flatter ourselves at having already reached these heights of clarity because we imagine we have left such phantoms of gods far behind. But what we have outgrown are only the word-ghosts, not the psychic facts which were responsible for the birth of the gods. We are still as possessed by our autonomous psychic contents as if they were gods. To-day they are called phobias, compulsions, and so forth, or in a word, neurotic symptoms. The gods have become diseases; Zeus no longer rules Olympus but the solar plexus, and creates specimens for the physician's consulting room, or disturbs the brains of the politicians and journalists who then unwittingly unleash mental epidemics.

So it is better for Western man if at the start he does not know too much about the secret insight of Eastern wise men, for it would be a case of the 'right means in the hands of the wrong man'. Instead of allowing himself to be convinced once more that the daemon is an illusion, the Westerner ought again to experience the reality of this illusion. He ought to learn to recognize these psychic forces again, and not wait until his moods, nervous states, and hallucinations make clear to him in the most painful way possible that he is not the only master in his house. The products of the disassociation tendencies are

[1] Mutze, Leipzig.

actual psychic personalities of relative reality. They are real when they are not recognized as such and are therefore projected; relatively real when they are related to the conscious (in religious terms, when a cult exists); but they are unreal to the extent that consciousness has begun to detach itself from its contents. However, this last is the case only when life has been lived so exhaustively, and with such devotedness, that no more unfulfilled obligations to life exist, when, therefore, no desires that cannot be sacrificed unhesitatingly stand in the way of inner detachment from the world. It is futile to lie to ourselves about this. Wherever we are still attached, we are still possessed; and when one is possessed, it means the existence of something stronger than oneself. ('Truly from thence thou wilt ne'er come forth until thou hast paid the last farthing.') It is not a matter of indifference whether one calls something a 'mania' or a 'god'. To serve a mania is detestable and undignified, but to serve a god is decidedly more meaningful and more productive because it means an act of submission to a higher, spiritual being. The personification enables one to see the relative reality of the autonomous psychic fragmentary system, and thus makes its assimilation possible and depotentiates the forces of fate. Where the god is not acknowledged, ego-mania develops, and out of this mania comes illness.

The teaching of yoga takes acknowledgement of the gods for granted. Its secret instruction is therefore intended only for him whose light of consciousness is on the point of disentangling itself from the powers of fate, in order to enter into the ultimate undivided unity, into the 'centre of emptiness', where 'dwells the god of utmost emptiness and life', as our text says. 'To hear such a teaching is difficult to attain in thousands of aeons.' Clearly the veil of maya cannot be lifted by a mere decision of reason, but demands the most thoroughgoing and persevering preparation consisting in the full payment of all debts to life. For as long as unconditional attachment through *cupiditas* exists, the veil is not lifted and the heights of a consciousness free of contents and free of illusion are not reached; nor can any trick nor any deceit bring this about. It is an ideal that can be completely realized only in death. Until then there are real and relatively real figures of the unconscious.

2. ANIMUS AND ANIMA

According to our text, among the figures of the unconscious there are not only gods but also the animus and anima. The word *hun* is translated by Wilhelm as animus. Indeed, the concept 'animus' seems appropriate for *hun*, the character for which is made up of the character for 'clouds' and that for 'demon'. Thus *hun* means 'cloud-demon', a higher 'breath-soul' belonging to the yang principle and therefore masculine. After death, *hun* rises upward and becomes *shen*, the 'expanding and self-revealing' spirit or god. 'Anima', called *p'o*, and written with the characters for 'white' and for 'demon', that is, 'white ghost', belongs to the lower, earth-bound, bodily soul, the yin principle, and is therefore feminine. After death, it sinks downward and becomes *kuei* (demon), often explained as the 'one who returns' (i.e. to earth), a revenant, a ghost. The fact that the animus and the anima part after death and go their ways independently shows that, for the Chinese consciousness, they are distinguishable psychic factors which have markedly different effects, and, despite the fact that originally they are united in 'the one effective, true human nature', in the 'house of the Creative', they are two. 'The animus is in the heavenly heart.' 'The animus lives in the daytime in the eyes (that is in consciousness); at night it houses in the liver.' It is that 'which we have received from the great emptiness, that which is identical in form with the primal beginning'. The anima, on the other hand, is the 'energy of the heavy and the turbid'; it clings to the bodily, fleshly heart. 'Desires and impulses to anger' are its effects. 'Whoever is sombre and moody on waking . . . is fettered by the anima.'

Many years ago, before Wilhelm acquainted me with this text, I used the concept 'anima'[1] in a way quite analogous to the Chinese definition of *p'o*, and of course entirely apart from any metaphysical premise. To the psychologist, the anima is not a transcendental being but something quite within the range of experience. For as the Chinese definition also makes clear, affective conditions are immediate experiences. But why then does one speak of anima and not simply of moods? The reason is that affects have an autonomous character, and therefore most people are under their power. But, as we have seen, affects are delimitable contents of consciousness, parts of the personality. As parts of the personality, they partake of its character and can therefore be easily personified, a process which is still going on to-day, as the examples cited above have shown. The personification is not an idle invention, inasmuch as the individual stirred by affect does not show a neutral character, but a quite distinct one, different from his ordinary character. Careful investigation has shown that the affective character in a man has feminine traits. This psychological fact has given rise to the Chinese teaching of the *p'o*-soul, as well as to my concept of the anima. Deeper introspection, or ecstatic experience, reveals the existence of a feminine figure in the unconscious, therefore the feminine name, anima, psyche, or soul. The anima can also be defined as an imago, or archetype, or as the resultant of all the experiences of man with woman. This is the reason the anima, as a rule, is projected on the woman. As we know, poetry has often described and celebrated the anima.[2]

[1] I refer the reader to the comprehensive presentation in my book, *Two Essays on Analytical Psychology*. (Translated by R. F. C. Hull, Bollingen Series XX, London and New York, 1953. C. F. B.)

[2] *Psychological Types*, chapter v, London and New York, 1923.

The connection of anima with ghost in the Chinese concept is of interest to parapsychologists inasmuch as the 'controls' are very often of the opposite sex.

Although Wilhelm's translation of *hun* as 'animus' seems justified to me, none the less I had important reasons for choosing 'logos' for a man's spirit, for masculine clarity of consciousness and reason, rather than the otherwise appropriate expression 'animus'. Chinese philosophers are spared certain difficulties which burden Western psychologists, because Chinese philosophy, like all mental and spiritual activity of ancient times, is exclusively a constituent of the masculine world. Its concepts are never taken psychologically, and have therefore never been examined as to how far they also apply to the feminine psyche. But the psychologist cannot possibly ignore the existence of woman and her special psychology. The reasons I prefer to translate *hun* as it appears in man by logos are connected with this fact. Wilhelm in his translation uses logos for the Chinese concept *hsing*, which could also be translated as essence [of human nature], or creative consciousness. After death, *hun* becomes *shen*, spirit, which is very close, in the philosophical sense, to *hsing*. Since the Chinese concepts are not logical in our sense, but are intuitive ideas, their meaning can only be fathomed through the ways in which they are used, and by noting the constitution of the written characters, or further, by such relationships as that of *hun* to *shen*. *Hun*, then, would be the discriminating light of consciousness and of reason in man, originally coming from the *logos spermatikos* of *hsing*, and returning after death through *shen* to the Tao. For this use, the expression 'logos' ought to be especially appropriate, since it includes the idea of a universal being, and therefore covers the fact that man's clarity of consciousness and capacity for reason are universal rather than something individually unique; moreover it is not personal, but in the deepest sense impersonal, and thus in sharp contrast to the anima, which is a personal demon expressing itself in thoroughly personal moods (therefore animosity!).

In consideration of these psychological facts, I have reserved the term 'animus' for women exclusively, because, to answer a famous question, '*mulier non habet animam, sed animum*'. Feminine psychology contains an element analogous to the anima of man. Primarily, it is not of an affective nature but is a quasi-intellectual element best described by the word 'prejudice'. The conscious side of woman corresponds to the emotional side of man, not to his 'mind'. Mind makes up the 'soul', or better, the 'animus' of woman, and just as the anima of the man consists of inferior relatedness, full of affect, so the animus of woman consists of inferior judgements, or better said, opinions. (For further details I must refer the reader to my essay cited above, for here I can only touch upon the general aspects.) The animus of woman consists in a plurality of preconceived opinions, and is therefore not so susceptible of personification by one figure, but appears more often as a group or crowd. (A good example of this from parapsychology is the so-called 'Imperator' group in the case of Mrs. Piper.)[1] On a low level, the animus is an inferior logos, a caricature of the differentiated masculine mind, just as the anima, on a low level, is a caricature of the feminine eros. Following the parallelism further, we can say that just as *hun* corresponds to *hsing*, translated by Wilhelm as logos, so the eros of woman corresponds to *ming*, which is translated as fate, *fatum*, destiny, and is interpreted by Wilhelm as eros. Eros is an interweaving; logos is differentiating knowledge, clarifying light; eros is relatedness; logos is discrimination and detachment. Thus the inferior logos in the woman's animus appears as something quite unrelated, and therefore as an inaccessible prejudice, or as an opinion which, irritatingly enough, has nothing to do with the essential nature of the object.

[1] Compare Hyslop, *Science and a Future Life*, Boston, 1905.

I have often been reproached for personifying the anima and animus as mythology does, but this reproach would be justified only if it were proven that in my psychological use of these terms I concretize them in the same way that mythology does. I must declare once and for all that the personification is not an invention of mine, but is inherent in the nature of the phenomena. It would be unscientific to overlook the fact that the anima is a psychic, and therefore a personal, autonomous system. None of the people who make the charge against me would hesitate a second to say: 'I dreamed of Mr. X', whereas, strictly speaking, he only dreamed of the representation of Mr. X. The anima is nothing but a representation of the personal nature of the autonomous system in question. What the nature of this autonomous system is in a transcendental sense, that is to say, beyond the boundaries of experience, we cannot know.

I have defined the anima in man as a personification of the unconscious in general, and have therefore taken it to be a bridge to the unconscious, that is, to be the function of relationship to the unconscious. There is an interesting point in our text in this connection. The text says that consciousness (that is, personal consciousness) comes from the anima. Since the Western mind is based wholly on the standpoint of consciousness, it must define anima in the way I have done, but the East, based as it is on the standpoint of the unconscious, sees consciousness as an effect of the anima! Without a doubt, consciousness originally arises out of the unconscious. This is something we forget too often, and therefore we are always attempting to identify the psyche with consciousness, or at least attempting to represent the unconscious as a derivative, or an effect of the conscious (as, for example, in the Freudian repression theory). But for the reasons discussed above, it is essential that nothing be taken away from the reality of the unconscious, and that the figures of the unconscious should be understood as active quantities. The person who has understood what is meant by psychic reality need have no fear that he has fallen back into primitive demonology. If indeed the unconscious figures are not taken seriously as spontaneously active factors, we become victims of a one-sided faith in the conscious mind, which finally leads to a state of over-tension. Catastrophes are then bound to occur, because, despite all our consciousness, the dark psychic powers have been overlooked. It is not we who personify them; they have a personal nature from the very beginning. Only when this is thoroughly recognized can we think of depersonalizing them, that is of 'subjugating the anima', as our text expresses it.

Here again we find a great difference between Buddhism and our Western attitude of mind, and again there is a dangerous semblance of agreement. Yoga teaching rejects all fantasy contents and we do the same, but the East does it on quite different grounds. In the East, conceptions and teachings prevail which express the creative fantasy in richest measure; in fact, protection is required against the excess of fantasy. We, on the other hand, look upon fantasy as valueless, subjective day-dreaming. Naturally the figures of the unconscious do not appear as abstractions stripped of all imaginative trappings; on the contrary, they are embedded and interwoven in a web of fantasies of extraordinary variety and bewildering abundance. The East can reject these fantasies because long ago it extracted their essence and condensed it in profound teachings. But we have never even experienced these fantasies, much less extracted their quintessence. Here we have a large portion of experience to catch up with, and only when we have found the sense in apparent nonsense can we separate the valuable from the worthless. We may rest assured that what we extract from our experiences will differ from what the East offers us to-day. The East came to its knowledge of inner things in relative ignorance of the external world. We, on the other hand, will investigate the psyche and its depths supported by a tremendously extensive historical and scientific knowledge. At this present moment, it is true, knowledge of the external world is the greatest obstacle to introspection, but the psychological distress will overcome all obstructions. We are already building up a psychology, that is, a science which gives us a key to things to which the East has found entrance, only through abnormal psychic states.

THE DETACHMENT OF CONSCIOUSNESS
FROM THE OBJECT

BY UNDERSTANDING the unconscious we free ourselves from its domination. This is really also the purpose of the instructions in our text. The pupil is taught to concentrate on the light of the inmost region and, while doing so, to free himself from all outer and inner entanglements. His life-impulse is guided towards a consciousness without content which none the less permits all contents to exist. The *Hui Ming Ching* says about this detachment:

> 'A halo of light surrounds the world of the law.
> We forget one another, quiet and pure, altogether
> powerful and empty.
> The emptiness is irradiated by the light of the heart
> of heaven.
> The water of the sea is smooth and mirrors the moon
> in its surface.
> The clouds disappear in blue space; the mountains
> shine clear.
> Consciousness reverts to contemplation; the moon-
> disk rests alone.'

This description of fulfilment pictures a psychic state which perhaps can best be characterized as a detachment of consciousness from the world, and a withdrawal of it to an extra-mundane point, so to speak. Thus consciousness is at the same time empty and not empty. It is no longer preoccupied with the images of things but merely contains them. The fullness of the world which heretofore pressed upon consciousness has lost none of its richness and beauty, but it no longer dominates consciousness. The magical claim of things has ceased because the original interweaving of consciousness with the world has come to an end. The unconscious is no longer projected, and so the primal *participation mystique* with things is abolished. Therefore consciousness is no longer preoccupied with compulsive intentions but turns into contemplative vision, as the Chinese text very aptly says.

How did this effect come about? (We assume, of course, that the Chinese author was first of all not a liar; secondly, that he was of sound mind; and, thirdly, that he was an extraordinarily intelligent man.) To understand or explain the detachment described in the text our mentality requires a somewhat roundabout approach. There is no use in our mimicking Eastern sensibility; for nothing would be more childish than to wish to aestheticize a psychic condition such as this. This detachment is something I am familiar with in my practice; it is the therapeutic effect *par excellence*, for which I labour with my students and patients, that is, the dissolution of *participation mystique*. With a stroke of genius, Lévy-Bruhl[1] has established *participation mystique* as being the hallmark of primitive mentality. As described by him it is simply the indefinitely large remnant of non-differentiation between subject and object, still so great among primitives that it cannot fail to strike European man, identified as he is with the conscious standpoint. In so far as the difference between subject and object does not become conscious, unconscious identity prevails. The unconscious is then projected into the object, and the object is introjected into the subject, that is, psychologized. Plants and animals then behave like men; men are at the same time themselves and animals also, and everything is alive with ghosts and gods. Naturally, civilized man regards himself as

[1] *Primitive Mentality*, London, 1923.

immeasurably above these things. Instead, often he is identified with his parents throughout his life, or he is identified with his affects and prejudices, and shamelessly accuses others of the things he will not see in himself. In a word, even he is afflicted with a remnant of primal unconsciousness, or non-differentiation between subject and object. By virtue of this unconsciousness, he is held in thrall by countless people, things, and circumstances, that is, unconditionally influenced. His mind, nearly as much as the primitive's, is full of disturbing contents and he uses just as many apotropaeic charms. He no longer works the magic with medicine bags, amulets, and animal sacrifices, but with nerve remedies, neuroses, 'progress', the cult of the will, and so forth.

But if the unconscious can be recognized as a co-determining quantity along with the conscious, and if we can live in such a way that conscious and unconscious, or instinctive demands, are given recognition as far as possible, the centre of gravity of the total personality shifts its position. It ceases to be in the ego, which is merely the centre of consciousness, and instead is located in a hypothetical point between the conscious and the unconscious, which might be called the self. If such a transposition succeeds, it results in doing away with *participation mystique*, and a personality develops that suffers only in the lower stories, so to speak, but in the upper stories is singularly detached from painful as well as joyful events.

The creation and birth of this superior personality is what is meant by our text when it speaks of the 'holy fruit', the 'diamond body', or refers in other ways to an indestructible body. These expressions are psychologically symbolical of an attitude which is out of reach of intense emotional involvement and therefore safe from absolute shock; they symbolize a consciousness detached from the world. I have reasons for believing that this sets in after the middle of life and is actually a natural preparation for death. To the psyche death is just as important as birth and, like it, is an integral part of life. What happens to the detached consciousness in the end is a question the psychologist cannot be expected to answer. Whatever theoretical position he assumed, he would hopelessly overstep the boundaries set him by science. He can only point out that the views of our text with respect to the timelessness of the detached consciousness are in harmony with the religious thought of all times, and with the thought of the overwhelming majority of mankind. A person thinking differently would stand outside the human order in some way, and therefore would be suffering from a disturbed psychic equilibrium. Thus, as a physician, I make a great effort to fortify the belief in immortality as far as I can, especially in my older patients, for whom such questions are crucial. If viewed correctly in the psychological sense, death is not an end but a goal, and therefore life towards death begins as soon as the meridian is passed.

The Chinese philosophy of yoga is based upon the fact of this instinctive preparation for death as a goal, and, following the analogy with the goal of the first half of life, namely, begetting and reproduction, the means towards perpetuation of physical life, it takes as the purpose of spiritual existence the symbolic begetting and bringing to birth of a psychic spirit-body ('subtle body'), which ensures the continuity of the detached consciousness. It is the pneumatic man, known to the European from antiquity, which he, however, seeks to produce by quite other symbols and magical practices, by faith and a Christian way of life. Here again we stand on a foundation quite different from that of the East. Again the text sounds as though it were not very far from Christian ascetic morality, but nothing could be more mistaken than to assume that it is actually dealing with the same thing. Back of our text is a culture thousands of years old, one which has built organically upon primitive instincts and which, therefore, knows nothing of the arbitrary morality violating the instincts characteristic of us as recently civilized

Teutonic barbarians. For this reason the Chinese are without that impulse towards violent repression of the instincts which hysterically exaggerates and poisons our spirituality. The man who lives his instincts can also detach from them, and in just as natural a way as he lived them. Any idea of heroic self-conquest would be entirely foreign to the sense of our text, but that is what it certainly would amount to if we followed the Chinese instructions literally.

We must never forget our historical premises. Only a little more than a thousand years ago we stumbled from the crudest beginnings of polytheism into the midst of a highly developed Oriental religion which lifted the imaginative minds of half-savages to a height that did not correspond to their degree of spiritual development. In order to maintain this height in some fashion or other, the instinctual sphere inevitably had to be repressed to a great extent. Thus religious practice and morality took on a markedly violent, almost malicious, character. The repressed elements naturally do not develop, but vegetate further in their original barbarism in the unconscious. We would like to scale the heights of a philosophical religion but are, in fact, incapable of it. To grow up to it is the most we can hope for. The Amfortas wound and the Faustian split in the Germanic man are not yet healed; his unconscious is still loaded with those contents which must first become conscious before he can be liberated from them. Recently I received a letter from a former patient which pictures the necessary transformation in simple but pertinent words. She writes: 'Out of evil, much good has come to me. By keeping quiet, repressing nothing, remaining attentive, and by accepting reality—taking things as they are, and not as I wanted them to be—by doing all this, unusual knowledge has come to me, and unusual powers as well, such as I could never have imagined before. I always thought that when we accepted things they over-powered us in some way or other. This turns out not to be true at all, and it is only by accepting them that one can assume an attitude towards them.[1] So now I intend to play the game of life, being receptive to whatever comes to me, good and bad, sun and shadow that are forever alternating, and, in this way, also accepting my own nature with its positive and negative sides. Thus everything becomes more alive to me. What a fool I was! How I tried to force everything to go according to the way I thought it ought to!'

Only on the basis of such an attitude, which renounces none of the values won in the course of Christian development, but which, on the contrary, tries with Christian charity and forbearance to accept even the humblest things in oneself, will a higher level of consciousness and culture be possible. This attitude is religious in the truest sense, and therefore therapeutic, for all religions are therapies for the sorrows and disorders of the soul. The increasing development of Western intellect and will has given us an almost fiendish capacity for aping such an attitude, with apparent success, despite the protests of the unconscious. But it is only a matter of time until the counter position forces recognition of itself one way or another. Aping an attitude always produces an unstable situation, which can be overthrown by the unconscious at any time. A safe foundation is found only when the instinctive premises of the unconscious win the same consideration as the viewpoints of the conscious mind. There can be no doubt that this necessity of giving due consideration to the unconscious runs violently counter to the Occidental and particularly to the Protestant cult of consciousness. Yet, though the new always seems the enemy of the old, anyone with a more than superficial desire to understand cannot fail to discover that without the most serious application of the Christian values we have acquired, the new integration can never take place.

---

[1] Dissolution of *participation mystique*.

THE FULFILMENT

GROWING ACQUAINTANCE with the spiritual East should be no more to us than the symbolical expression of the fact that we are entering into connection with the elements in ourselves which are still strange to us. Denial of our own historical premises would be sheer folly and would be the best way to bring about another deracination. Only by standing firmly on our own soil can we assimilate the spirit of the East.

Describing people who do not know where the true springs of secret powers lie, an ancient adept says: 'Worldly people lose the roots and cling to the tree-tops.' The spirit of the East has come out of the yellow earth, and our spirit can, and should, come only out of our own earth. It is for this reason that I approach these problems in a way that has often been criticized as being 'psychologism'. If 'psychology' were meant, I should be flattered, because it is really my purpose to push aside without mercy the metaphysical claims of all esoteric teaching; the secret objective of gaining power through words ill accords with our profound ignorance—which we should have the modesty to confess. It is my firm intention to bring things which have a metaphysical sound into the daylight of psychological understanding, and to do my best to prevent the public from believing in obscure words of power. Let the convinced Christian believe, for that is the duty he has taken upon himself. The non-Christian has forfeited the grace of faith. (Perhaps he was cursed from birth in not being able to believe, but only to know.) Therefore, he has no right to put his faith elsewhere.

One cannot grasp anything metaphysically, but it can be done psychologically. Therefore I strip things of their metaphysical wrappings in order to make them objects of psychology. In this way I can at least extract something understandable from them, and can avail myself of it. Moreover, I learn to know psychological conditions and processes which before were veiled in symbols and out of reach of my understanding. In doing this I also may be able to follow a similar path and to have similar experiences; if finally there should still be an ineffable metaphysical element, it would have the best opportunity of revealing itself.

My admiration for the great Eastern philosophers is as genuine as my attitude towards their metaphysics is irreverent.[1] I suspect them of being symbolical psychologists, to whom no greater wrong could be done than to take them literally. If it were really metaphysics that they mean, it would be useless to try to understand them. But if it is psychology, we can not only understand them, but we can profit greatly by them, for then the so-called 'metaphysical' comes within the range of experience. If I accept the fact that a god is absolute and beyond all human experience, he leaves me cold. I do not affect him, nor does he affect me. But if I know that a god is a powerful impulse of my soul, at once I must concern myself with him, for then he can become important, even unpleasantly so, and even in practical ways, which sounds horribly banal—like everything belonging to the sphere of reality.

The reproach of 'psychologism' applies only to a fool who thinks he has his soul in his pocket; there are certainly more than enough such fools, because, although we know how to use big words about the 'soul', the depreciation of psychic things

---

[1] The Chinese philosophers—in contrast to the dogmatists of the West— are only grateful for such an attitude, because they also are masters of their gods. (R. W.)

is still a typical Western prejudice. If I make use of the concept 'autonomous psychic complex', my reader immediately comes up with the prejudice, 'nothing but a psychic complex'. How can we be so sure that the soul is 'nothing but'? It is as if we did not know, or else continually forgot, that everything of which we are conscious is an image, and that image *is* psyche. The people who think God is depreciated if He is understood as something moved in the psyche, as well as the moving force of the psyche, that is, understood as an 'autonomous complex' —these same people can be so afflicted by uncontrollable affects and neurotic states of mind that their wills and their whole philosophy of life fail miserably. Is that proof of the impotence of the psyche? Should Meister Eckhart also be reproached with 'psychologism' when he says 'God must be brought to birth in the soul again and again'? I think the accusation of 'psychologism' is justified only in the case of the type of intellect which denies the nature of the autonomous complex, and seeks to explain it rationally as the consequence of known causes, that is, as derived, as not existing in its own right. This latter judgement is just as arrogant as the 'metaphysical' assertion which, overstepping human limitations, seeks to entrust a deity outside the range of our experience with the bringing about of our psychic states. 'Psychologism' is simply the counterpart of metaphysical encroachment, and just as childish as the latter. Therefore it seems to me far more reasonable to accord the psyche the same validity as the empirical world, and to admit that the former has just as much 'reality' as the latter. As I see it, the psyche is a world in which the ego is contained. Perhaps there are also fishes who believe that they contain the sea. We must rid ourselves of this habitual illusion of ours if we wish to consider metaphysical statements from the standpoint of psychology.

A metaphysical assertion of this kind is the idea of the 'diamond body', the indestructible breath-body which develops in the Golden Flower, or in the square inch space.[1] This body, like everything else, is a symbol for a remarkable psychological fact, which, because it is objective, first appears projected in forms born of the experiences of organic life, that is, as fruit, embryo, child, living body, and so on. This psychological fact could best be expressed in the words 'It is not I who live, it lives me.' The illusion as to the superior powers of the conscious leads to the belief: I live. If the recognition of the unconscious shatters this illusion, the former appears as something objective in which the ego is included. The attitude towards the uncon-

[1] True, our text is somewhat unclear as to whether by 'continuation of life' a survival after death or a prolongation of physical existence is meant. Expressions such as 'elixir of life' and the like are deceptively ambiguous. Indeed, it is evident in the later additions that the yoga instructions are also understood in a purely physical sense. To a more primitive mind, there is nothing disturbing in this odd mixture of the physical and the spiritual, because to it life and death are by no means the complete opposites they are to us. (Particularly interesting in this connection, besides the well-known ethnological material, are the 'communications' of the English 'rescue circles' with their thoroughly archaic ideas.) The same ambiguity with respect to survival after death is present in early Christianity also, where it depends on similar assumptions, that is, on the idea of a 'breath-body', the essential carrier of life. (Geley's parapsychological theory would be the latest reincarnation of this ancient idea.) But since in our text we also have warnings against superstitious use of it, for example, warnings against trying to make gold, we can confidently insist without contradiction to the sense of the text on the spiritual meaning of the instructions. In the conditions which the instructions seek to produce, the physical body plays an increasingly inessential rôle because it is replaced by the 'breath-body' (hence the importance of breathing in yoga practice in general). The 'breath-body' is not 'spiritual' in our sense. It is characteristic of Western man that he has split apart the physical and the spiritual sides of life for the purpose of gaining knowledge, but these opposites exist together in the psyche, and psychology must recognize the fact. 'Psychic' means physical *and* mental. The ideas in our text all deal with this 'in-between' world which seems unclear and confused to us because the concept of psychic reality is not yet current among us, although it defines our sphere of life. Without soul, mind is as dead as matter, because both are artificial abstractions; whereas man originally regarded mind as a volatile body, and matter as not lacking in soul.

scious is then analogous to the feeling of the primitive to whom the existence of a son guarantees continuation of life. This characteristic feeling can assume grotesque forms even, as in the case of the old Negro who, angered at his disobedient son, cried out: 'There he stands with my body, but does not even obey me!'

It is a question of a change in inner feeling similar to that experienced by a father to whom a son has been born; it is a change also known to us through the testimony of the Apostle Paul: 'Not I (live), but Christ liveth in me.' The symbol 'Christ' as the 'son of man' is an analogous psychic experience: a higher, spiritual being of human form is invisibly born in the individual, a spiritual body, which is to serve us as a future dwelling, a body which, as Paul expresses himself, is put on like a garment ('For as many of you as have been baptized into Christ have put on Christ'). Obviously it is always a difficult thing to express, in intellectual terms, subtle feelings which are, none the less, infinitely important for the life and well-being of the individual. In a certain sense, the thing we are trying to express is the feeling of having been 'replaced', but without the connotation of having been 'deposed'. It is as if the direction of the affairs of life had gone over to an invisible centre. Nietzsche's metaphor, 'in most loving bondage, free',[1] would be appropriate here. Religious speech is full of imagery picturing this feeling of free dependence, of calm and devotion.

In this remarkable experience I see a phenomenon resulting from the detachment of consciousness, through which the subjective 'I live' becomes the objective 'It lives me'. This state is felt to be higher than the earlier one; it is really as if it were a sort of release from compulsion and impossible responsibility which are the inevitable results of *participation mystique*. This feeling of liberation fills Paul completely. It is the consciousness

[1] *'Frei in liebevollstem Muss.'*

of being a child of God which frees one from the spell of the blood. It is also a feeling of reconciliation with all that happens, and that is the reason that, according to the *Hui Ming Ching*, the glance of one who has attained fulfilment returns to the beauty of nature.

In the Pauline Christ symbol the deepest religious experiences of the West and of the East confront each other. Christ the sorrow-laden hero, and the Golden Flower that blooms in the purple hall of the city of jade—what a contrast, what an infinity of difference, what an abyss of history! A problem fit for the crowning work of a future psychologist!

Among the great religious problems of the present is one which has received scant attention, but which, in fact, is the main problem of our day: the problem of the progress of the religious spirit.[1] If we are to discuss it, we must emphasize the difference between East and West in their treatment of the 'jewel', that is, the central symbol. The West emphasizes the human incarnation, and even the personality and historicity of Christ, while the East says: 'Without beginning, without end, without past, without future.'[2] In accordance with his conception, the Christian subordinates himself to the superior, divine person in expectation of His grace; but the Eastern man knows that redemption depends on the 'work' the individual does upon himself. The Tao grows out of the individual. The *imitatio Christi* has this disadvantage: in the long run we worship as a divine example a man who embodied the deepest meaning of life, and then, out of sheer imitation, we forget to make real our own deepest meaning—self-realization. As a matter of fact, it is not altogether uncomfortable to renounce one's own real meaning. Had Jesus done this, He would probably have become a respectable carpenter, and not the religious rebel to

[1] For the sake of clarity the author amplified the above sentence for the English translation. (C. F. B.)

[2] *Hui Ming Ching*, p. 77.

whom, obviously, there would happen to-day the same thing that happened then.

Imitation of Christ might well be understood in a deeper way. It might be taken as the duty to give reality to one's deepest conviction, always the fullest expression of individual temperament, with the same courage and the same self-sacrifice shown by Jesus. Happily—we must say—not everyone has the task of being a leader of mankind, or a great rebel, and so it might be possible for each to realize himself in his own way. This honesty might even become an ideal. Since great innovations always begin in the most unlikely places, the fact, for example, that a person to-day is not nearly as ashamed of his nakedness as he used to be might be the beginning of a recognition of himself as he is. Hard upon this will follow an increasing recognition of many things that were formerly strictly taboo, because the reality of the earth will not forever remain veiled like the *virgines velandae* of Tertullian. Moral unmasking is only one step further in the same direction, and behold, there stands a man as he is, and confesses to himself that he is as he is. If he does this in a meaningless way he is a muddled fool, but if he knows the significance of what he does he can belong to a higher order of man who makes real the Christian symbol, regardless of suffering. It can often be observed that wholly concrete taboos or magical rites in an early stage of a religion become in the next stage a matter of psychic concern, or even wholly spiritual symbols. An external law, in the course of time, becomes an inner conviction. Thus it might easily happen to contemporary man, especially the Protestant, that the person Jesus, now existing outside in the realm of history, might become the superior man within himself. Then we would have attained, in a European way, the psychological state corresponding to 'enlightenment' in the Eastern sense.

All this is a step in the evolution of a higher human consciousness on the way towards unknown goals, and is not metaphysics in the ordinary sense. Thus far it is only 'psychology', but also thus far it can be experienced, it is intelligible, and—thank God—it is real, a reality with which something can be done, a reality containing possibilities and therefore alive. The fact that I content myself with what can be psychically experienced, and reject the metaphysical, does not mean, as anyone with insight can understand, a sceptic or agnostic gesture against faith or trust in higher powers; what I am saying is approximately the same thing Kant meant when he called 'the thing in itself' a 'merely negative boundary-concept' [*Grenzbegriff*]. Every statement about the transcendental is to be avoided because it is invariably only a laughable presumption on the part of the human mind, which is unconscious of its limitations. Therefore, when God or the Tao is termed an impulse of the soul, or a state of the soul, something has been said about the knowable only, but nothing about the unknowable, about which nothing can be determined.

CONCLUSION

THE PURPOSE of my commentary is to attempt to build a bridge of psychological understanding between East and West. The basis of every real understanding is man, and therefore I had to speak of human things. This must be my excuse for having dealt only with general aspects, and for not having entered into technical details. Technical directions are valuable for those who know, for example, what a camera is, or a combustion engine, but they are useless for anyone who has no idea of such apparatus. Western man for whom I write is in an analogous position. Therefore it seemed to me important above all to emphasize the agreement between the psychic states and symbolisms of East and West. By means of these analogies an entrance is opened to the inner chambers of the Eastern mind, an entrance that does not require the sacrifice of our own nature and hence does not threaten us with being torn from our roots. Nor is it an intellectual telescope or microscope offering a view fundamentally of no concern to us because it does not touch us. It is rather an atmosphere of suffering, seeking, and striving common to all civilized peoples; it is the tremendous experiment of becoming conscious, which nature has laid upon mankind, and which unites the most diverse cultures in a common task.

Western consciousness is by no means consciousness in general; it is a historically conditioned and geographically limited factor, representative of only one part of mankind. The widening of our consciousness ought not to proceed at the expense of other kinds of consciousness, but ought to take

1. ♀ The Golden Flower represented as the most splendid of all flowers.

2. ♀ In the centre, the Golden Flower; radiating out from it, fishes as fertility symbols (corresponding to the thunderbolts of the Lamaist mandalas).

3. ♂ A luminous flower in the centre, with stars rotating about it. Around the flower, walls with eight gates. The whole conceived as a transparent window.

4. ♀ Separation of the air-world and the earth-world. (Birds and serpents.)
In the centre a flower with a golden star.

5. ♀ Separation of the light from the dark world; the heavenly from the earthly soul. In the centre a representation of contemplation.

6. ♂ In the centre, the white light, shining in the firmament; in the first circle, protoplasmic life-seeds; in the second, rotating cosmic principles which contain the four primary colours; in the third and fourth, creative forces working inward and outward. At the cardinal points, the masculine and feminine souls, both again divided into light and dark.

7. ♀ Representation of the *tetraktys* in circular movement.

8. ♀ A child in the germinal vesicle with the four primary colours included in the circular movement.

9. ♀ In the centre, the germinal vesicle with a human figure nourished by blood vessels which have their origin in the cosmos. The cosmos rotates around the centre, which attracts its emanations. Around the outside is spread nerve tissue indicating that the process takes place in the solar plexus.

10. ♂ A mandala as a fortified city with wall and moat. Within, a broad moat
surrounded by a wall, fortified with sixteen towers and with another inner moat.
The latter moat surrounds a central castle with golden roofs whose centre is a
golden temple.

place through the development of those elements of our psyche which are analogous to those of the alien psyche, just as the East cannot do without our technology, science, and industry. The European invasion of the East was a deed of violence on a grand scale, and it has left us the duty—*noblesse oblige*—of understanding the mind of the East. This is perhaps more necessary than we realize at present.

EXAMPLES OF EUROPEAN MANDALAS

The pictures between pages 136 and 137 have been made by patients as described in the text. The earliest picture dates from 1916. All the pictures have been done independently of any Eastern influence. The *I Ching* hexagrams in picture No. 4 come from the reading of Legge's translation in the Sacred Books of the East Series but they were put into the picture only because their content seemed, to the university-trained patient, especially meaningful for her life. No European mandalas known to me (I have a fairly large collection) achieve the conventionally and traditionally established harmony and perfection of the Eastern mandala. I have made a choice of ten pictures from among an infinite variety of European mandalas, and they ought, as a whole, to illustrate clearly the parallelism between Eastern philosophy and the unconscious mental processes in the West.

C. G. JUNG

IN MEMORY OF RICHARD WILHELM[1]

By C. G. Jung

IT IS NO EASY TASK for me to speak of Richard Wilhelm and his work, because, starting very far away from one another, our ways crossed in a comet-like fashion. His life-work has a range which I have not encompassed. Nor have I seen the China that first shaped and later continued to engross him; moreover, I am not familiar with its language, the living spiritual expression of the Chinese East. I stand, indeed, as a stranger outside the vast territory of knowledge and experience in which Wilhelm worked as a master of his profession. He, as a Sinologue, and I, as a physician, would probably never have come into contact had we remained specialists. But we met in a field of humanity which begins beyond academic boundary posts. There lay our point of contact; there leaped across the spark that kindled the light destined to become for me one of the most meaningful events of my life. Because of this experience I may speak of Wilhelm and his work, thinking with grateful reverence of this mind which created a bridge between East and West and gave to the Occident the precious heritage of a culture thousands of years old, a culture perhaps destined to disappear.

Wilhelm possessed the mastership which is won only by the man who surmounts his specialty, and so his knowledge became a concern touching all humanity, or rather it was that at the

[1] This memorial address was delivered in Munich, May 10, 1930. It was not published in conjunction with *The Secret of the Golden Flower* in German until the current edition, the fifth, in 1957. There were one or two sentences and phrases in the German text made available to me in 1930 which do not appear in the German text of this fifth edition. They have not been removed from the revised translation which follows. (C. F. B.)

beginning and remained so always. For what else could have liberated him so completely from the narrow horizon of the European, of the missionary, in fact, so that no sooner had he encountered the secret of the Chinese soul than he perceived the treasure hidden there for us, and sacrificed his European prejudice on behalf of this rare pearl? It could only have been an all-embracing humanness, a greatness of heart that divines the whole, which enabled him to open himself without reservation to a profoundly foreign spirit, and to put at the services of this influence the manifold gifts and capacities of his mind. Reaching beyond all Christian *ressentiment*, beyond all European presumption, his comprehending devotion is in itself witness of a rarely great spirit, for all mediocre minds in contact with a foreign culture lose themselves either in blind self-deracination or in an equally uncomprehending, as well as presumptuous, passion for criticism. Touching only the surface and externals of the foreign culture, they never eat its bread nor drink its wine, and so never enter into the *communio spiritus*, that most intimate transfusion and interpenetration which prepares a new birth.

As a rule, the specialist's is a purely masculine mind, an intellect to which fecundity is an alien and unnatural process; therefore it is an especially ill-adapted tool for receiving and bringing to birth a foreign spirit. But a greater mind bears the stamp of the feminine; to it is given a receptive and fruitful womb which can reshape what is strange into a familiar form. Wilhelm possessed in the highest degree the rare charism of spiritual motherhood. To it he owed his as yet unequalled ability to make incomparable translations.

To me the greatest of his achievements is the translation of, and commentary on, the *I Ching*.[1] Before I came to know

---

[1] *The I Ching or Book of Changes*. The Richard Wilhelm translation rendered into English by Cary F. Baynes. Bollingen Series XIX, London and New York, 1950.

Wilhelm's translation, I had for years worked with Legge's inadequate rendering, and was therefore in a position to recognize fully the extraordinary difference between the two. Wilhelm has succeeded in bringing to life again, in a new and vital form, this ancient work in which not only many Sinologues but even many modern Chinese as well can see nothing but a collection of absurd magical formulae. This work embodies, as perhaps no other, the spirit of Chinese culture, for the best minds of China have collaborated upon it and contributed to it for thousands of years. Despite its fabulous age, it has never grown old, but still lives and operates, at least for those who understand its meaning. That we too belong to this favoured group we owe to the creative effort of Wilhelm. He has brought this work close to us through careful translation and through his personal experience both as a pupil of a Chinese master of the old school and as an initiate in the psychology of Chinese yoga, to whom the practical application of the *I Ching* was a constantly renewed experience.

But with all these rich gifts, Wilhelm has also burdened us with a task whose magnitude we may at the moment only guess at, but cannot fully visualize. Anyone who, like myself, has had the rare good fortune to experience in a spiritual exchange with Wilhelm the divinatory power of the *I Ching*, cannot for long remain ignorant of the fact that we have touched here an Archimedean point from which our Western attitude of mind could be shaken to its foundations. It is no small service to have given us, as Wilhelm did, such an all-embracing, richly coloured picture of a foreign culture; but much more important is the fact that he has transmitted to us the living germ of the Chinese spirit, capable of working an essential change in our view of life. We are no longer reduced to being admiring or critical observers, but have become participants in the Eastern spirit, to the degree to which we have succeeded in experiencing the effective potency of the *I Ching*.

The function on which the use of the *I Ching* is based at first sight appears to be in sharp contradiction to our Western way of scientific causal thinking. In other words, it is extremely unscientific, in fact taboo, and therefore outside the scope of our scientific judgement, indeed incomprehensible to it.

Some years ago, the then president of the British Anthropological Society asked me how I could explain the fact that so highly intellectual a people as the Chinese had produced no science. I replied that this must really be an optical illusion, because the Chinese did have a 'science' whose 'standard work' was the *I Ching*, but that the principle of this science, like so much else in China, was altogether different from our scientific principle.

The science of the *I Ching*, indeed, is not based on the causality principle, but on a principle (hitherto unnamed because not met with among us) which I have tentatively called the synchronistic principle. My occupation with the psychology of unconscious processes long ago necessitated my casting around for another explanatory principle, because the causality principle seemed to me inadequate for the explanation of certain remarkable phenomena of the unconscious. Thus I found that there are psychic parallelisms which cannot be related to each other causally, but which must stand in another sort of connectedness. This connection seemed to me to lie mainly in the relative simultaneity of the events, therefore the expression 'synchronistic'. It seems, indeed, as though time, far from being an abstraction, is a concrete continuum which contains qualities or basic conditions manifesting themselves simultaneously in various places in a way not to be explained by causal parallelism, as, for example, in cases of the coincident appearance of identical thoughts, symbols, or psychic states. Another example would be the simultaneity of Chinese and European periods of style, a fact pointed out by Wilhelm. They could not have been causally related to one another. Astrology would be an excellent example of manifest synchronicity if it had at its disposal thoroughly tested findings. But at least there are some facts thoroughly tested and backed up by a wealth of statistics which make the astrological problem seem worthy of philosophical investigation. (Psychology has no difficulty in recognizing this, since astrology represents the summation of all the psychological knowledge of antiquity.)

The fact that it is possible to reconstruct in adequate fashion a person's character from the data of his nativity shows the relative validity of astrology. However, the birth-data never depend on the actual astronomical constellations, but upon an arbitrary, purely conceptual time-system, because by reason of the precession of the equinoxes the spring point has long ago passed on beyond zero degree Aries. In so far as there are any really correct astrological diagnoses, they are not due to the effects of the constellations but to our hypothetical time-qualities. In other words, whatever is born or done in this moment of time has the quality of this moment of time.

This is also the basic formula for the use of the *I Ching*. One gains knowledge of the hexagram characterizing the moment by a method of manipulating yarrow stalks, or coins, a method depending on sheer chance. As the moment is, so do the runic stalks fall. The only question is: Did the old King Wen and the Duke of Chou, a thousand years before Christ, interpret correctly the accidental picture made by the fallen stalks? As to this, experience alone can tell.

At his first lecture at the Psychological Club in Zürich, Wilhelm, at my request, demonstrated the method of consulting the *I Ching* and, at the same time, made a prognosis which, in less than two years, was fulfilled to the letter and with unmistakable clearness. This fact could be further confirmed by many parallel experiences. However, I am not concerned here with establishing objectively the validity of the prophecies of the *I Ching*, but take it as a premise, just as my deceased friend did. Therefore, I am only going to discuss the amazing fact that the *qualitas occulta* of the time-moment became legible by means of the hexagram of the *I Ching*. One is dealing with the relationship of events, not only analogous to astrology, but even essentially related to it. The moment of birth corresponds to the stalks that are thrown, the constellation to the hexagram, and the astrological interpretation arising from the constellation corresponds to the text allocated to the hexagram.

The type of thought built on the synchronistic principle, which reached its apex in the *I Ching*, is the purest expression of Chinese thinking in general. In the West this thinking has been absent from the history of philosophy since the time of Heraclitus, and only reappears as a faint echo in Leibnitz. However, in the interim it was not extinguished, but continued to live in the twilight of astrological speculation, and remains to-day at this level.

At our point of time the *I Ching* responds to the need of further development in us. Occultism has enjoyed a renaissance in our times which is virtually without a parallel. The light of the Western mind is nearly darkened by it. I am not thinking now of our seats of learning and their representatives. I am a physician and deal with ordinary people, and therefore I know that the universities have ceased to act as disseminators of light. People have become weary of scientific specialization and rationalistic intellectualism. They want to hear truths which broaden rather than restrict them, which do not obscure but enlighten, which do not run off them like water, but penetrate them to the marrow. This search threatens to lead a large, if anonymous, public into wrong paths.

When I think of Wilhelm's achievement and significance, I am always reminded of Anquetil-Duperron, the Frenchman who brought the first translation of the Upanishads to Europe at the very period when, after almost eighteen hundred years, an unheard-of thing happened: the goddess of reason drove the Christian Godhead from the throne in Notre Dame. To-day, when far more unheard-of things happen in Russia than once did in Paris, when in Europe itself the Christian symbol shows such weakness that even the Buddhists consider this the right moment for sending missions to Europe, it is Wilhelm, representing as he does the soul of Europe, who brings us new light from the East. This was the cultural task to which Wilhelm felt himself called. He had realized how much the East could give for the healing of our spiritual distress.

A poor man is not helped by having more or less generous alms pressed upon him, although this may be his wish. He is much better helped if we show him how, by work, he can free himself permanently of his need. Unfortunately, the spiritual beggars of our time are too inclined to accept the alms of the East in specie, that is, to appropriate unthinkingly the spiritual possessions of the East and to imitate its way blindly. That is the danger about which it is impossible to give too many warnings, and the one which Wilhelm also felt very vividly. Spiritual Europe is not helped by what is merely a new sensation or a new titillation of the nerves. What it has taken China thousands of years to build cannot be grasped by theft. We must instead earn it in order to possess it. What the East has to give us should be merely help in a work which we still have to do ourselves. Of what use to us is the wisdom of the Upanishads or the insight of Chinese yoga, if we desert the foundations of our own culture as though they were errors outlived and, like homeless pirates, settle with thievish intent on foreign shores? The insights of the East, above all, the wisdom of the *I Ching*, have no meaning when we close our minds to our own problems, when we veil from ourselves our real human nature with all its dangerous undercurrents and darknesses. The light of this wisdom shines only in the dark, not in the glaring searchlight of the European theatre of consciousness and will.

The wisdom of the *I Ching* originated from a background whose horror we can faintly suspect if we read of Chinese massacres, of the sinister power of Chinese secret societies, of the nameless misery, the hopeless filth and vices, of the Chinese masses.

We need to have a correctly three-dimensional life if we wish to experience Chinese wisdom as a living thing. Therefore, we first have need of European truths about ourselves. Our way begins in European reality and not in yoga practices which would only lead us astray as to our own reality. We must continue Wilhelm's work of translation in a wider sense if we wish to show ourselves worthy pupils of the master. Just as he translated the spiritual treasure of the East into European meaning, we should translate this meaning into life.

Wilhelm translated the central concept, the Tao, as 'meaning'. To translate meaning into life, that is to realize the Tao, would be the task of the pupil. But the Tao will never be created with words and wise precepts. Do we know exactly how the Tao develops in us or around us? Is it by imitation, by reason, by acrobatics of the will? We feel that all this is ridiculously incommensurate with the task. But where shall we begin with this next task? Will Wilhelm's spirit be in us or with us if we do not solve this problem in a truly European way—that is, in reality? Or must this, in the last analysis, remain a rhetorical question whose answer is lost in applause?

Let us look towards the East: there an overwhelming fate is fulfilling itself. European cannon have burst open the gates of Asia; European science and technology, European secularism and greed flooded China. We have conquered the East politically. Do you know what happened when Rome overthrew the Near East politically? The spirit of the East entered Rome. Mithra became the Roman military god, and out of the most unlikely corner of Asia Minor came a new spiritual Rome. Would it be unthinkable that the same thing might happen to-day and find us just as blind as were the cultured Romans who marvelled at the superstitions of the *Christoi*? It is to be noted that England and Holland, the two main colonizing powers in Asia, are also the two most infected with Hindu theosophy. I know that our unconscious is full of Eastern symbolism. The spirit of the East is really at our gates. Therefore it seems to me that the translation of meaning into life, the search for the Tao, has already become a collective phenomenon among us, and that to a far greater extent than is generally realized. A most significant sign of the times, it seems to me, is that Wilhelm and the Indologue Hauer were asked to lecture on yoga at this year's congress of German psychotherapists. Let us realize what it means for a practising physician who deals directly with a suffering, and therefore receptive, person, to establish contact with an Eastern therapeutic system. Thus the spirit of the East penetrates through all our pores and reaches the most vulnerable places of Europe. It could be a dangerous infection, but perhaps it is also a remedy. The Babylonian confusion of tongues in the West has created such a disorientation that everyone longs for simpler truths, or at least for general ideas which speak, not to the head alone, but to the heart as well, which give clarity to the contemplating mind and peace to the restless pressure of the feelings. Like ancient Rome, we again to-day are importing every form of exotic superstition in the hope of discovering therein the right remedy for our disease.

Human instinct knows that all great truth is simple, and therefore the man who is weak in instinct assumes great truth to exist in all cheap simplifications and platitudes. Or, as a result of his disappointment, he falls into the opposite error of thinking that great truth must be as obscure and complicated as possible. We have to-day a Gnostic movement in the anonymous masses which exactly corresponds psychologically with the Gnostic movement nineteen hundred years ago. Then, as to-day, solitary wanderers like the great Apollonius spun the spiritual threads from Europe back to Asia, perhaps to remotest India.

Looked at from such a historical perspective, I see Wilhelm in the guise of one of those great Gnostic intermediaries who brought the cultural heritage of Asia Minor into contact with the Hellenic spirit, and thereby caused a new world to rise out of the ruins of the Roman Empire. Then, as now, the continent of the spirit was inundated, leaving only single peaks projecting like islands from the limitless flood. Then, as now, all sorts of devious paths beckoned the mind and the wheat of false prophets flourished.

In the midst of the jarring disharmony of European opinion, to hear the simple language of Wilhelm, the messenger from China, is indeed a blessing. It has obviously been schooled in the plant-like spontaneity of the Chinese mind, which is able to express profound things in plain language; it discloses something of the simplicity of great truth and of deep meaning. It has transplanted in the soil of the West a tender seedling, the Golden Flower, giving us a new intuition of life and meaning, as a relief from the tension of arbitrary will and arrogance.

Faced with the alien culture of the East, Wilhelm showed a degree of modesty highly unusual in a European. He approached it freely, without prejudice, without the assumption of knowing better; he opened heart and mind to it. He let himself be gripped and shaped by it, so that when he came back to Europe he brought us not only in his spirit but also, in his being, a true image of the East. This deep transformation was certainly not won by him without great sacrifice, for our historical premises are so entirely different from those of the East. The keenness of Western consciousness and its glaring problems had to soften before the more universal, more equable nature of the East; Western rationalism and its one-sided differentiation had to yield to Eastern breadth and simplicity. To Wilhelm, this change certainly meant not only a shifting of intellectual standpoint, but also an essential rearrangement of the component parts of his personality. The picture of the East that he has given us, free as it is of purposefulness and any trace of arbitrariness, could never have been created in such completeness if Wilhelm had not been able to let the European in himself slip into the background. If he had allowed East and West to clash within him with unyielding harshness, he would have failed in his mission of providing us with a true picture of China. The sacrifice of the European man was unavoidable and necessary for the fulfilment of the task fate laid upon him.

Wilhelm fulfilled his mission in the highest sense of the word. Not only did he make accessible to us the past treasures of the Chinese mind, but, as I have pointed out, he brought with him its spiritual root, the root that has remained alive all these thousands of years, and planted it in the soil of Europe. With the completion of this task, his mission reached its climax and, unfortunately, its end also. According to the law of *enantiodromia*, so clearly understood by the Chinese, there grew out of the close of the one phase the beginning of its opposite. Thus, in its culmination, yang goes over into yin, and what had been positive becomes negative. I came near to Wilhelm only in the last years of his life, and then I could observe how, with the completion of his life-work, Europe and the European man impinged ever more closely on him, oppressed him in fact. At the same time, there developed in him the feeling that he might be standing on the brink of a great change, a revolution whose nature, it is true, he could not clearly grasp. He only knew that he faced a decisive crisis. His physical illness went parallel with this spiritual development. His dreams were filled with Chinese memories, but the pictures hovering before him were always sad and dismal, a clear proof that the Chinese contents had become negative.

Nothing can be sacrificed forever. Everything returns later

in a changed form, and where so great a sacrifice has once taken place, when the sacrificed thing returns, it must be met by a still healthy and resistant body in order to take the shock of a great revolution. Therefore, a spiritual crisis of such dimensions often means death if it takes place in a body weakened by disease. For now the sacrificial knife is in the hand of him who has been sacrificed, and a death is demanded of him who was once the sacrificer.

As you see, I have not withheld my personal ideas, because if I had not told how I experienced Wilhelm, how else would it have been possible for me to speak of him? Wilhelm's life-work is of such great value to me because it explained and confirmed so much of what I had been seeking, striving for, thinking and doing, in order to meet the psychic suffering of Europe. It was a tremendous experience for me to hear through him, in clear language, the things that had been dimly shadowed forth to me from out of the confusion of the European unconscious. In fact, I feel myself so very much enriched by him that it seems to me as if I had received more from him than from any other man, and this is also the reason I do not feel it a presumption if I am the one to offer on the altar of his memory the gratitude and respect of all of us.